PRIDE

CELEBRATING DIVERSITY & COMMUNITY

Robin Stevenson

ORCA BOOK PUBLISHERS

Library and Archives Canada Cataloguing in Publication

Stevenson, Robin, 1968–, author
Pride: celebrating diversity & community / Robin Stevenson.

Includes index.

Issued in print and electronic formats.
ISBN 978-1-4598-0993-2 (paperback).—ISBN 978-1-4598-0994-9 (pdf).—
ISBN 978-1-4598-0995-6 (epub)

1. Gay Pride Day—Juvenile literature. 2. Gay pride celebrations—Juvenile literature.
3. Gay liberation movement—Juvenile literature. I. Title.
HQ76.5.S74 2016   j306.76'6   C2015-904526-6
                           C2015-904527-4

First published in the United States, 2016
Library of Congress Control Number: 2015946192

Summary: This work of nonfiction for middle readers examines what—and why—gay, lesbian, bisexual and transgender people and their supporters celebrate on Pride Day every June.

Orca Book Publishers is dedicated to preserving the environment and has printed this book on Forest Stewardship Council® certified paper.

Orca Book Publishers gratefully acknowledges the support for its publishing programs provided by the following agencies: the Government of Canada through the Canada Book Fund and the Canada Council for the Arts, and the Province of British Columbia through the BC Arts Council and the Book Publishing Tax Credit.

Design by Rachel Page
Front cover photography by Tony Sprackett
Back cover photography by Jen MacLellan, Tony Sprackett, iStock.com, Dreamstime.com, Shutterstock.com
Lyrics to "Rise Up" courtesy of Lorraine Segato/ Lynne Fernie/Lauri Conger/
Steve Webster/ Billy Bryans, Sony ATV Publishing

ORCA BOOK PUBLISHERS
www.orcabook.com

Printed and bound in Canada.

19 18 17 16 • 4 3 2 1

To my parents, Ilse and Giles; my partner, Cheryl; and my son, Kai, with love and gratitude. And to all the LGBTQIA+ kids and families out there—I wish you many happy Pride Days.

In memory of Kenneth Gerard Rogers (1954–1990)

CONTENTS

The EuroPride Parade in Oslo, Norway, in June 2014. Nanisimova/Dreamstime.com

INTRODUCTION

For gay, lesbian, bisexual and transgender people and their supporters, June is a month of pride and celebration, and the high point of that month is the Pride parade.

I went to my first Pride parade when I was still in high school. It was in Toronto, in the late 1980s. These days, Toronto's Pride celebration is one of the biggest in the world, but back then it was much smaller. It felt huge to me though! I was enthralled by the beautifully decorated floats, the extravagant costumes and the music, and I was blown away by the sight of thousands of people dancing in the streets. I felt as if I had entered a magical world—one in which everyone could truly be themselves.

I began attending Pride as a teenager because I had gay friends and I wanted to support them. A few years later,

A group of people in New York City show their support for Pride. isogood/iStock.com

A small child watches the Pride parade in Victoria, BC. Tony Sprackett

Sometimes my family marches in the Pride parade and other years we watch from the sidelines. In this photo, my son, my partner and I are sitting in front of the British Columbia Legislature and waiting for the parade to go by. Robin Stevenson

I came out as a lesbian and went right on attending Pride events as a proud member of the queer community. More than twenty years later, it is still a day I look forward to every year.

Now when I go to Pride celebrations, it is in Victoria, British Columbia, with my partner and our eleven-year-old son. He was only a month old at his first Pride Day, and he hasn't missed a year since. His favorite part when he was small? Balloons, ice cream and an excuse to dress up!

Pride Day is a spectacular and colorful event. But there is a whole lot more to Pride than rainbow flags and amazing outfits. So what exactly *are* we celebrating on Pride Day? How did this event come to be? And what does Pride mean to the people who celebrate it? Keep reading to find out!

A child waves a Pride flag during a Pride parade in London, England. Chris Harvey/Shutterstock.com

THE HISTORY OF PRIDE

IN THE BEGINNING

To understand the beginnings of Pride, you need to understand a bit of history. The world has not always been an easy place for men who love other men, women who love other women, and people who don't conform to traditional ideas about gender. In many ways, and in many parts of the world, this is still true—but here in North America, we really have come a long way.

Back in the 1950s, lesbians, gay men, bisexuals and transgender people (or LGBT people for short) did not have equal rights in Canada or the United States. It wasn't just that they couldn't get married—same-sex relationships were actually considered a crime! LGBT people didn't have legal protection from discrimination, so they could be evicted from their homes and fired from their jobs simply for

Chicago Pride Parade. Sianamira/Dreamstime.com

Activist Barbara Gittings, founder of the New York City chapter of the Daughters of Bilitis, picketing the White House in 1965.
Kay Tobin Lahusen/Wikipedia

being who they were. Restaurants and bars could refuse to serve them. They could be arrested by police for being in gay bars or nightclubs, or for dancing with a same-sex partner.

But whenever there is oppression, there is resistance. People fight back—and that's how change happens.

FIGHTING BACK

One of the earliest gay organizations in the United States was the Mattachine Society, started in 1950 by a small group of gay men in Los Angeles. It was named for a group of masked medieval performers—a reference to the fact that gay men in the 1950s were forced to live behind masks, keeping their relationships secret. The men who joined the Mattachine Society in those early days also had another dangerous secret to keep: many of them had links to the Communist Party, and at that time, being a Communist could cost you your job—or even land you in jail.

A few years later, in 1955, two women called Del Martin and Phyllis Lyon gathered together eight lesbian women in San Francisco. They wanted a social group—and a place that group could talk and dance together without risking arrest. Like members of the Mattachine Society, they had to be secretive, and most members didn't even use their real names. They called their organization the Daughters of Bilitis, after a fictional lesbian character in an obscure poem. If anyone asked, they could say they were just a poetry club!

The groups quickly grew in numbers and became less secretive—and more political. In 1965, an activist named Craig Rodwell came up with an idea that led to some of the first public demonstrations by LGBT people: the Annual Reminders. Starting in July 1965, small groups of courageous activists picketed Philadelphia's Independence Hall each year, to remind Americans that LGBT people did not have basic civil rights. The first of these demonstrations had almost forty people marching, including members of the Mattachine Society and the Daughters of Bilitis. They carried signs to let everyone know what they wanted: *15 MILLION HOMOSEXUAL AMERICANS ASK FOR EQUALITY, OPPORTUNITY, DIGNITY.*

And momentum was building across the country. During the late 1960s, pickets and other protests also took place in New York, Washington, DC, Chicago, Los Angeles and San Francisco.

Gay rights demonstration in New York City, 1976.
Leffler, Warren K/Wikipedia

GAY IS GOOD

One of the early American civil rights activists who took part in the Annual Reminders was Frank Kameny. In 1957, Kameny was fired from his government job for being gay. He was one of many Americans who lost their jobs during this era, because government officials thought gay and lesbian employees were vulnerable to blackmail by Communists. This fear, and the resulting persecution of thousands of gay men and lesbians during the 1950s and '60s, has been called the Lavender Scare. During this time, the Canadian government also attempted to identify

"Gay is Good" bumper sticker. DCVirago/Flickr

QUEER FACT

BISEXUAL ACTIVIST BRENDA HOWARD has been called the Mother of Pride. She was involved in the Stonewall Riots and continued to be a hardworking activist throughout her life. As a member of the Christopher Street Liberation Day committee, she came up with the idea of naming the days leading up to the march Gay Pride Week. Brenda actively promoted the use of the word *pride* to describe these events.

Frank Kameny attending Capital Pride in Washington DC, in June 2010. The Pride Parade route included a street recently been renamed "Frank Kameny Way" in his honor. David/Flickr

and eliminate gay men and lesbians from the civil service, the military and the police force.

Frank Kameny decided not to accept this treatment, and he sued the US government in federal court. It was a battle that went on for eighteen years, through appeal after appeal, and it gained a huge amount of publicity for the growing gay rights movement. Ultimately, Frank Kameny lost the lawsuit—but he helped to win the larger battle for gay rights. He started a Washington, DC, chapter of the Mattachine Society and kept on fighting. In 1975, after a number of lawsuits, the government's anti-gay policy was finally changed. Today, there are openly gay employees at every level of government.

Activists like Frank Kameny not only helped change policy, but they also fought to change attitudes. In the 1950s and '60s, many believed being gay or lesbian was a mental illness.

Activists argued against this idea, pointing out recent research published in two books called *The Kinsey Reports*. This groundbreaking research into a taboo subject showed that same-sex relationships were far more common than had previously been thought. Activists used the research in *The Kinsey Reports* as the basis for their statement that at least 10 percent of the population was gay or lesbian—and this was very significant in helping to shift public opinion.

In 1960s America, a cultural movement known as "Black is Beautiful" was taking hold and challenging long-held racist ideas. Inspired by this, Frank Kameny coined the slogan "Gay is Good" in 1968. It was an attempt to counter the shame often felt by LGBT people living in such hostile times. "Gay is Good" was a move away from secrecy—and toward Pride.

HOW PRIDE DAY BEGAN WITH A RIOT

In the 1960s, there weren't many public places where LGBT people could gather. New York, which had one of the largest gay populations in North America, actually had a law that made it illegal for restaurants and bars to serve them. It was illegal for a man to dance with another man—or to wear clothing intended for the opposite sex! A woman could be arrested if she was wearing fewer than three pieces of "feminine clothing," and a man could be jailed for wearing a dress. Police regularly raided and shut down gay bars, arresting staff and customers.

One popular gay bar in New York was called the Stonewall Inn. It was on Christopher Street in Greenwich

My friends Khalilah and Katie at a Pride parade in Victoria, BC. Their T-shirts read *The first Gay Pride was a riot!*—a reference to the 1969 riots at the Stonewall Inn. Tony Sprackett

"... the Stonewall Rebellion was the shot heard round the world... The gay liberation movement was an idea whose time had come. The Stonewall Rebellion was crucial because it sounded the rally for the movement. It became an emblem for gay and lesbian power."

—Lillian Faderman, historian and author of Odd Girls and Twilight Lovers

Stonewall Inn, site of the 1969 Stonewall Riots, New York City, USA. On the window: *We homosexuals plead with our people to please help maintain peaceful and quiet conduct on the streets of the Village.* —Mattachine, New York Public Library/ Wikipedia

Village, and it was owned by the Mafia. The manager, known as Fat Tony, bribed the police with monthly payments so that they would turn a blind eye. It wasn't a fancy place—in fact, it didn't even have running water— but it was one of very few places where LGBT people could dance, chat, listen to music and be themselves.

Police raids weren't unusual at the Stonewall Inn, even with Fat Tony's bribes. Usually a few arrests were made, the bar shut down and reopened for business a few hours later. But on the evening of June 28, 1969, something was different. As police arrested customers and began taking them to the paddy wagon, the crowd began to fight back.

As word of the demonstration spread throughout the city, the customers of the Stonewall Inn were soon joined by others from the gay, lesbian and transgender community. A crowd began to gather outside, shouting "Gay power" and throwing coins, bottles and bricks from a nearby construction site. It wasn't long before the police

QUEER FACT

IN MANY ACCOUNTS OF the Stonewall Riots, a transgender street kid called Sylvia Rivera is said to have thrown the first beer bottle at the police. But Sylvia Rivera's story doesn't begin or end with Stonewall. Sylvia was born as a boy named Ray, to Puerto Rican and Venezuelan parents, and raised in poverty by her grandmother. After conflicts related to her gender expression—she began wearing makeup in fourth grade—she left home to live on the streets at age ten. Poor, Hispanic, transgender, often homeless, Sylvia knew what it meant to be an outsider, and she spent her life fighting to make the world a better place for the most marginalized people in the LGBT community.

Sylvia was a founding member of the Gay Liberation Front and the Gay Activists Alliance, but as the gay rights movement became more mainstream, transgender people and drag queens often found themselves sidelined. Many activists seemed to focus on fitting in to the world, rather than changing it. Not Sylvia. She co-founded a group called STAR: Street Transvestite Action Revolutionaries, and did everything from marching for change to helping create shelters for street kids. A true revolutionary, she never stopped speaking her mind and fighting for the rights of street youth and transgender people of color.

lost control of the situation and had to barricade themselves inside the bar.

Riot officers were called in wearing helmets with visors and armed with nightsticks and tear gas, but the crowd refused to give up. The conflict between the police and the protestors lasted until the early hours of that morning, and riots broke out again the next night, and the next.

AFTER STONEWALL

Lesbian, gay, bisexual and transgender people had fought back against the police before the Stonewall Riots, but not so fiercely and not in such large numbers. The Stonewall Riots became a symbol of resistance and changed the movement from a small group of activists to a much bigger fight for change. New groups were formed, including the Gay Liberation Front and the Gay Activists Alliance, and a month after the riots, the first mass rally for gay rights took place in New York City. And it wasn't long before gay

In 2015, the Stonewall Inn was made a New York City landmark in recognition of its historical significance. NYC Pictures

"I'm glad I was in the Stonewall Riot...that's when I saw the world change for me and my people. Of course, we still got a long way ahead of us."

—Sylvia Rivera, drag queen, transgender activist, revolutionary (1951–2002)

"Before the riots I wanted to go around and convince the straight world we were okay. And after Stonewall we told the straight world that we didn't give a damn what they thought."

—Martha Shelley, American lesbian activist, feminist, writer and poet, born 1943

Members of the Gay Activists Alliance carry a sign in a 1971 gay rights march. Photo by Richard C. Wandel, courtesy LGBT Community center National History Archive

liberation marches began to spread across the country, the continent and the world.

Marches were an important part of all the social movements of the 1960s—the civil rights movement, the anti-war movement, the women's liberation movement and the youth liberation movement. It was a politically charged time. Activists who were organizing after Stonewall did not see gay rights as separate from other human rights issues. They saw connections between different forms of oppression, and they wanted to take action to make the world a better place for everyone.

Even though activists had been organizing for change for years, the Stonewall Riots are often seen as the beginning of the Pride movement. It was an important turning point for the community—so important, in fact, that people often refer to the 1950s and '60s as the pre-Stonewall era.

THE FIRST PRIDE PARADE

Although it wasn't yet called Pride Day, most people agree that the first Pride parade was held a year after the Stonewall Riots, on June 28, 1970. Activists declared it Christopher Street Liberation Day and organized the first ever gay rights march in New York City.

One of the organizers was Craig Rodwell, owner of the Oscar Wilde Memorial Bookshop on Christopher Street, the first gay bookshop in the country. Craig had been a member of the Mattachine Society, but he felt the organization was too conservative and that it was time for a bolder approach. The bookshop became a meeting place for a number of the newly formed activist groups, and its mailing list proved valuable in organizing the first ever gay

On June 28, 1970, one year after the Stonewall Riots, New York City had its first gay rights march.
Photo by Leonard Fink, courtesy LGBT Community Center National History Archive

rights march. After much discussion, the group chose a slogan for the marchers to chant: "Say it clear, say it loud. Gay is good, gay is proud!"

That same weekend, marches were also held in Chicago, Los Angeles and San Francisco. The following year, Canada's first Gay Day Picnic was held in Toronto. And by 1972, marches were being held in many cities across North America—and they were starting to pop up all over Europe too.

Most North American Pride events today are held on a weekend that falls close to June 28—the anniversary of the Stonewall Riots.

GROWING PAINS

Dropping the language of gay liberation and adopting the philosophy of gay pride represented a shift from protest

> *"Stonewall happens every day... When you go to a Pride March and you see people standing on the side of the road watching and then someone takes that first step off the curb to join the marchers, that's Stonewall all over again."*
>
> —*Virginia M. Apuzzo, American LGBT rights activist and educator, former executive director of the National Lesbian and Gay Task Force, born 1941*

A group of young activists at the 1970 gay rights march in New York City. Photo by Leonard Fink, courtesy LGBT Community Center National History Archive

In the early 1970s, activists in North America and Europe were forming groups and organizing protests, like this Gay Liberation Front demonstration in London, England. LSE Library/Flickr Commons

to celebration. Not everyone supported this change. Was Pride Day moving too far from its radical roots?

The LGBT community has always been diverse, and not everyone had the same political goals. Some people wanted to focus on the fight for the same rights that heterosexuals had, such as the right to marry. Others felt that we should embrace our differences from heterosexual, or straight, traditions, and that focusing on marriage equality was a mistake.

Another challenge to the growing Pride movement was the lack of equality *within* the community: sexism, racism and classism meant that while some voices were heard, others were silenced. Lesbians, who had fought alongside gay men from the beginning, were often invisible as male voices took center stage. Drag queens and people who didn't conform to traditional gender roles were marginalized by those who thought they should try to fit in by appearing more like straight people. People of color and anti-racism activists challenged the community to address the racism within its ranks. People living in poverty, including LGBT youth whose parents kicked them out of their homes, faced different concerns than wealthy people. People with disabilities pointed out that meetings and dances were regularly held in locations that weren't wheelchair accessible. Transgender people had long been allies to gays and lesbians, but the violence and discrimination they faced were rarely made a priority by gay and lesbian activists. Although great progress has been made, all of these issues continue to be problems today.

Pride has had some growing pains, but the central values of diversity, equality and freedom have been a

strong thread guiding the community through the decades of change. Still, just like any family, the community will probably continue to have its arguments.

That's part of how we learn—by challenging each other to grow.

Gay Vietnam Vets protesting the war—and demanding equal rights—in a 1972 gay rights march. Photo by Leonard Fink, courtesy LGBT Community center National History Archive

YOUTH ON THE FRONT LINES

Young people were very active in all the social movements of the 1960s. Universities and college campuses were intensely political, with demonstrations and strikes being regular occurrences. Student activists protested against racism, against the Vietnam War, against sexism. They organized to work for peace, equality and social justice. So it is not surprising that young people have been involved in fighting for change since the earliest days of the gay rights movement.

> *"It is not our differences that divide us. It is our inability to recognize, accept and celebrate those differences."*
>
> —Audre Lorde, black lesbian feminist, poet and activist (1934-1992)

A queer youth group marches in London's Pride Parade.
Chris Harvey/Shutterstock.com

"I wanted to start a GSA at my school because I knew that most teens have a much harder time coming out than I did."
—Carl Swanson at the Edmonton Pride Parade.
Ruby Swanson

The first high school-based activism started not long after Stonewall. In 1972, a group of students at New York City's George Washington High School got together and decided to organize for change. Soon other youth groups started to appear across the country.

Today, thousands of high schools and middle schools across North America have groups that offer support for LGBT students and allies, and provide opportunities to for them to meet each other. They also work to fight homophobia and make school a safer space for all students. These groups are often called Gay-Straight Alliances, or GSAs.

Alberta teenager Carl Swanson started a GSA at his high school in Edmonton. He had come out himself the summer before grade 12, and his family and close friends were very supportive. I asked Carl why he decided to start a GSA. He told me, "I remember thinking that people my age pretty much spent their time in three places: at home, with their friends and at school. If I set up a GSA at my school, I could guarantee that one of those three places would be safe and welcoming for students like me."

SILENCE = DEATH

The first Pride Days I attended were in the late 1980s, at the height of the AIDS epidemic. Although we now know that anyone can get AIDS, the first people in North America to develop the illness were gay men. Young, healthy men were suddenly getting sick and dying—and no one knew why. It was a terrifying and devastating time for people in the gay community. Thousands had already died, and many more were ill. One of those men was my close friend and housemate, Kenny.

In the 1980s, little was known about AIDS. There were no effective treatments—but there was a great deal of fear and terrible prejudice. Several of my friends from university stopped coming to my house when they found out that I lived with someone who had AIDS. Some health care providers actually refused to treat AIDS patients.

New York City hosts an annual Pride March that is one of the world's largest. The Pride March—sometimes referred to as the Pride Parade—passes the historically significant site of the Stonewall Inn on Christopher Street. isogood/iStock.com

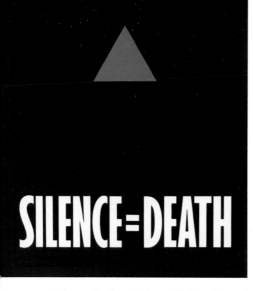

Silence = Death poster image. Wellcome Images/ Wikipedia

In the early years of the AIDS epidemic, LGBT communities in North American cities organized politically to fight against AIDS, homophobia and government inaction. The first Fighting for Our Lives march was a candlelight march in New York City, in 1983. Courtesy LGBT Community center National History Archive

By 1987, AIDS had spread to over a hundred countries—and more than twenty thousand people had died in the United States alone. And yet homophobia and indifference at the highest levels of government led to a shockingly inadequate official response.

But LGBT people and their supporters came together to fight for change. Using the slogan Silence = Death, a small group of gay activists in New York challenged the LGBT community to turn their fear, their anger and their grief into action, and in 1987 a new group called ACT UP was formed. ACT UP (AIDS Coalition to Unleash Power) and the LGBT community fought ignorance with education campaigns and fought discrimination in courtrooms across North America. They pressured governments, scientists and drug companies to do more research and to make new experimental treatments available.

And these activists were hugely successful. In fact, they deserve much of the credit for the existence of treatments that now make HIV/AIDS a manageable disease for many people in the world's wealthier nations.

The AIDS epidemic is tragic. It devastated the gay community in the 1980s and '90s, and it continues to destroy millions of lives in many countries around the world. But the fight against AIDS made the North American LGBT community stronger, more politically organized and more visible—which set the stage for the next wave of activism.

THE QUEER NINETIES

In 1990, AIDS activists from ACT UP founded a new group: Queer Nation. Queer Nation was a response to the violence, harassment and prejudice that LGBT people continued to face, and its mission was to eliminate homophobia and increase LGBT visibility. Queer Nation's name represented the reclaiming of the word *queer*. Activists took back a word that had been used against them, as an insult, and proudly owned it: queer included anyone whose gender or sexuality fell outside what was narrowly considered to be "normal." And the reclaiming was a success: LGBT became LGBTQ.

Queer Nation's tactics were direct and confrontational, and their message was clear: We're here, we're queer, and we're not going away! They held "Nights Out," in which queer participants would go to straight bars and night clubs and dance with same-sex partners. Queer Nation took their activism beyond the cities and into the suburbs, organizing a Queer Shopping Network and

Promotional material used by Queer Nation Houston. Wikipedia

Queer Nation logo by Alan MacDonald and Patrick Lilley from 1992. Wikipedia

A group of marriage equality supporters with signs in front of the US Supreme Court Building in Washington, DC. Purdue9394/iStock.com

traveling to malls to hand out flyers that read *We're here, we're queer and we'd like to say hello!* The flyers included information about LGBTQ people and a list of famous queers throughout history.

In June of 1990, hundreds of Queer Nation members in New York City marched in the city's Gay Pride parade behind a banner that read *Queer Nation…Get Used To It!*

EQUAL FAMILIES, EQUAL RIGHTS

When I came out as a lesbian in the early 1990s, lesbian and gay relationships were not recognized in Canadian law, and the *Canadian Human Rights Act* did not include protection from discrimination based on sexual orientation. But the AIDS epidemic had politicized the LGBTQ community, and more and more gay, lesbian, bisexual and transgender people were living their lives openly, creating families and demanding recognition and protection.

I was living in Ontario at the time and involved with a local activist group. The provincial government was discussing a proposed new law called Bill 167, or the *Equality Rights Statute Amendment Act, 1994*. It was the first attempt to pass legislation recognizing our relationships in Canada,

QUEER FACT

IN 1972, ACTIVISTS BARBARA GITTINGS and Frank Kameny spoke to the American Psychiatric Association to help educate psychiatrists about homosexuality. Many doctors still believed that homosexuality was a mental illness, so Barbara and Frank asked Dr. John Fryer, a gay psychiatrist, to join them. He agreed—but the climate was still so hostile for LGBT people that he felt he had to disguise himself. He wore a mask and used a special microphone to alter his voice and was introduced as Dr. H. Anonymous.

On the signs:

100% LESBIAN! But I'm still the person my parents raised me to be.

I am Proud to be in a Same-Sex relationship & when the day comes, I will be just as Proud to be her Wife!!

Incase you didn't notice- this is NOT a white flag! We will NOT Surrender!

Three marriage equality supporters hold signs across from the US Supreme Court Building in Washington, DC. Purdue9394 /iStock.com

and if it passed, same-sex couples would have the same rights and obligations as opposite-sex couples. It felt like we were on the verge of a historic victory.

We threw our energy into supporting Bill 167—organizing letter-writing campaigns, giving interviews on local radio stations, putting up posters and holding public demonstrations. But when the members of the government finally voted, the bill was defeated. In Toronto, protestors filled the visitors' gallery in the legislature building, crying, "Shame, shame!" before taking to the streets, where they blocked traffic and chanted, "We're here, we're queer, we all pay taxes."

Quebec couple Amy Stewart and Elena Abel got married in Nevada in 2015.
Trey Tomsik from Scenic Las Vegas Weddings

Ottawa couple Shelley Taylor and Natasha Coldevin.
Nathaniel Westley

At the time, I was devastated. How could anyone not see that our relationships—our families—needed recognition and protection? It was hard to accept that the government of my own country didn't think that we deserved the same rights everyone else had.

Bill 167 failed—but the LGBTQ community in the early 1990s really was on the verge of victory. The progress made in the years since that time has been remarkable.

In 2001, the Netherlands led the way, legalizing same-sex marriage. Belgium and Spain were quick to follow. In 2005, same-sex marriage was adopted in Canada. In the United States, recognition of same-sex marriage varied from state to state—making the fight for equality one that was fought on many fronts. Finally, in June 2015, a US Supreme Court ruling made same-sex marriage legal across the country.

Same-sex marriage is now legal in Canada, the United States, the United Kingdom, Ireland and many other European countries, as well as in Mexico, Argentina, Brazil, Uruguay, New Zealand and South Africa. A number of other countries recognize civil unions, which, while not considered marriage, give same-sex couples the same rights as married couples.

San Francisco Pride. Walleyelj/Dreamstime.com

Just as important, public opinion has also changed drastically. By coming out and living our lives openly, LGBTQ people have shown the world that we really are everywhere. And generally, people don't hate or fear what they know. Support for LGBTQ rights is higher than it has ever been.

However, all this progress may have provoked a backlash in some countries, which is something we'll explore in the last chapter.

PROUD MOMENTS

PARENTS UNITE!

Jeanne Manford, founder of PFLAG, takes part in a 1974 Pride march with a group of other parents. Photo by Leonard Fink, courtesy LGBT Community Center National History Archive

Morty Manford knew he was gay from the time he was a teenager, and as a young man in New York City, he joined the GAA—the Gay Activists Alliance. In 1972, while he was handing out leaflets to protest media oppression, Morty was attacked and beaten so badly that he was hospitalized for a week.

His mother, a schoolteacher named Jeanne Manford, was furious. "I'm very shy," she says. "I was not the type of person who belonged to organizations. But I wasn't going to let anybody walk over Morty."

She wrote a letter to the *New York Post*. "I mentioned that my son was gay and that the police stood by and watched these young gays being beaten up and did nothing." The letter was printed and soon everyone was talking about it. Jeanne was asked to be on a television show in Boston—and then in Cincinnati and New Orleans and Detroit. "I guess it was the first time a mother ever sat down and publicly said, 'Yes, I have a homosexual child.' I was never quiet about having a gay son. I'd tell strangers; I didn't care. I figured this was one way to educate people."

Later that year, Morty Manford asked his mother to march with him in the Christopher Street Liberation Day March. She agreed to join him—on one condition. "I'll march if you let me carry a sign," she told him.

She carried a sign that read *PARENTS OF GAYS: UNITE IN SUPPORT FOR OUR CHILDREN*. During the parade, Jeanne was amazed—and very moved—by the overwhelming emotional response of the crowd. People stood and applauded as she walked by, and many ran up to her, thanking her and hugging her. "As Morty and I walked along during that first march, we were talking about starting some kind of organization. So many people said, 'Talk to my parents,'" Jeanne recalls.

So Jeanne decided to start a support group for parents whose children were gay.

The first meeting was held at a church in New York's Greenwich Village. About twenty people came. And from that small group came PFLAG—Parents, Families and Friends of Lesbians and Gays. PFLAG went on to become an international organization that now has more than 200,000 members around the world.

Today, the sign that Jeanne Manford carried in the 1972 Pride parade is in the New York Public Library archives.

A parent marches in support of her gay son in a 1975 Pride march. Photo by Leonard Fink, courtesy LGBT Community Center National History Archive

"I felt that the love in my own home was more important than what others thought about me."

—Jeanne Manford, founder of PFLAG

QUEER FACT

IN 2014, THE MEMBERSHIP OF PFLAG VOTED to change the name of their organization from Parents, Families and Friends of Lesbians and Gays (for which PFLAG was an acronym) to PFLAG National. They wanted to keep the name that has become familiar to so many—but also to be more inclusive of the bisexual, transgender and queer members of the LGBTQ community.

Young and old, generations come together to celebrate diversity at a Pride Day picnic on Salt Spring Island, off the west coast of British Columbia. Flat Earth Photography

2

PRIDE AND IDENTITY

WHO GOES TO PRIDE EVENTS?

Pride is a celebration of diversity, equality and freedom—and everyone is welcome to enjoy it. The people who go to Pride Day parades and festivals include members of the queer community, their friends and family, people who support LGBTQ rights and believe in the importance of Pride celebrations, and many individuals and families who are looking for a fun and entertaining way to spend a day.

Seeing all the thousands of people supporting and celebrating Pride together was important to me when I first came out as a lesbian. It helped me realize that I was not alone, that I was part of a large, vibrant and exciting community. Knowing that so many others were choosing to

Three friends wait for the parade to pass by in Victoria, BC. Robin Stevenson

be visible—to be open about who they were, to hold hands and dance together in the streets, to have fun and celebrate, to demand acceptance and respect, to fight for equal rights—helped me find the courage to do the same.

FINDING COMMUNITY

You have probably grown up with a number of cultural celebrations, events and holidays. They may be connected to your religion, like Passover or Christmas or Diwali, or to the country your ancestors came from, like Chinese New Year or Scotland's Hogmanay or Mexico's *Dia de los Muertos* (Day of the Dead). These celebrations are part of your cultural heritage, shared by your family and your community.

But while some aspects of identity—like ethnicity, language and religion—are usually shared by all members of a family, others—like sexual orientation—are often not. Pride Day makes the LGBTQ community more visible. And that is important, especially for young people who might otherwise feel very alone.

My friend Tom grew up in a small town in the Maritimes in the 1950s—long before the Stonewall Riots and the first Pride parades. By age ten or eleven, he knew he was different. He knew he liked boys, but he didn't know that anyone else in the world felt the same way. He didn't have any words for how he felt, and he couldn't imagine telling anyone. The only explanation he could think of was that he came from another planet. And every night he stared out his bedroom window, watching the sky and waiting for a spaceship to come and take him back to his own world. He was confused and desperately unhappy. A Pride parade—even if he didn't attend it, even if it wasn't

Celebrating Pride in Vancouver, BC. Tony Sprackett

in his town, even if he only heard about it or saw pictures in a newspaper—would have let him know that he was not alone. It would have let him know that people like him existed and could be happy and proud of who they were.

WHAT IS COMING OUT?

Most heterosexual teens don't have to think too much about what sex they are attracted to or whether to tell their parents—and the majority of kids don't question whether they are a boy or a girl. For LGBTQ teens, though, this part of life is often more complicated. It is very common during the teen years, and sometimes much earlier, for questions about sexual orientation and identity to surface.

Coming out refers to the process LGBTQ people go through as they move toward understanding and accepting

EuroPride Parade in Oslo, Norway.
Nanisimova/Shutterstock.com

their gender identity or sexual orientation. It also refers to sharing that understanding with other people in their lives—for example, talking openly with their friends or family about their identity, their personal feelings or their romantic relationships. Coming out can be a gradual process, and many people choose to come out only to a few close friends at first. Others are comfortable being very open about who they are.

Coming out is a very personal decision and one that no one should be pressured into making. It can be scary to come out to people, especially if you aren't sure how they will react. If you are too young to live independently and you suspect your parents will not be supportive, coming out to your family may be too risky. Happily, the world

Flags, dresses, ribbons, leggings, umbrellas, and even hair...You can't go wrong with rainbow-themed accessories at a Pride Festival. Tony Sprackett

is changing, and while homophobic attitudes are still a problem, they are becoming less and less common. And there is a lot of support out there!

If you are thinking about coming out, or supporting a friend who is, there are some resources at the end of this book that you might find useful.

WHAT GROUPS MAKE UP THE QUEER COMMUNITY?

LGBTT2SQQIAA…Help! Sometimes people joke about our community's ever-evolving attempt to name itself. And yes, it does look a bit like alphabet soup! One acronym you might see is QUILTBAG: Queer/Questioning, Undecided, Intersex, Lesbian, Trans (Transgender/Transsexual), Bisexual, Asexual, Gay/Genderqueer. A shorter acronym that is sometimes used is GSM: Gender and Sexual Minorities. When you have a community made up of people who have often been excluded or invisible, you want to create a space where everyone feels welcome, seen and included. So finding inclusive language is important.

In this book, I often use the shorter version LGBTQ, or just the word *queer*. *Queer* is an umbrella term often used to encompass all the people in our diverse community,

New York City Pride. Kobby Dagan/Shutterstock.com

A very young supporter gets a ride and waves a Pride flag in a Los Angeles Pride parade.
shalunts/Shutterstock.com

QUEER FACT

OCTOBER 11 IS NATIONAL COMING OUT DAY, an annual holiday to celebrate coming out and to support LGBTQ people who have not yet done so. National Coming Out Day has been held every year since 1988. Why October 11? It is the anniversary of the 1987 National March on Washington for Lesbian and Gay Rights, a day on which half a million people marched on Washington, DC, in support of gay rights.

New York City Pride March. Stu99/Dreamstime.com

and I like it, but not everyone does. For some people—especially older gay men and lesbians who lived through less accepting times—the word is too strongly associated with memories of taunts and aggression. For others, reclaiming and embracing the word for our own use is itself a sign of pride. So it is complicated. In general, it is best to refer to people using the language that they choose to use for themselves. And if you aren't sure, ask!

LGBTT2SQQIAA... UNDERSTANDING THE QUEER ALPHABET

Lesbians are women who are primarily attracted to other women.

Gay refers to people who are attracted primarily to members of the same sex.

B stands for **bisexual** (sometimes just called **bi**). Bisexuals are people who are attracted to both men and women. Some people also use the word **pansexual**, meaning attracted to *all* genders, which recognizes that not everyone identifies as a man or a woman.

Transgender doesn't refer to **sexual orientation** (that's who you are attracted to) but to **gender identity**—your

QUEER FACT

ARE YOU CISGENDER? If you've never really questioned your gender identity—if you and everyone else have just always taken it for granted that you are a boy or a girl—then you probably are. Cisgender refers to people whose gender identity matches the sex they are assigned at birth. For example, a cisgender woman is a woman who was identified as female at birth, has lived her life as female and sees herself as a woman. Because they are part of a majority, most cisgender people don't think much about their gender identity—and don't even know the word!

Proud to be Trans! Salt Spring Island Pride Parade. Flat Earth Photography

internal sense of being male or female. This term is often used to refer to all people who do not identify with their assigned gender at birth (for example, someone who was identified as a girl when they were born but has always felt like a boy). This term also includes those whose gender identity lies outside of the idea of gender as **binary** (that is, either male or female). They may feel that they are neither male nor female, or that their identity lies somewhere between, beyond or outside. Some use the term **genderqueer** or **non-binary** instead of transgender. Others use the term **genderfluid**, to describe a gender identity that shifts from day to day.

Transexual is a term used by some transgender people who have **transitioned** from male to female or female to male.

> "I'm fighting for the abolition of apartheid. And I fight for the right of freedom of sexual orientation. These are inextricably linked with each other. I cannot be free as a black man if I am not free as a gay man."
>
> —Simon Nkoli, speaking at South Africa's first Pride parade, Johannesburg, October 13, 1990

A group of First Nations people drum their way through Vancouver's downtown streets in a Pride parade on Canada's west coast. Tony Sprackett

"The word 'queer' translates in Spanish to being 'rare.' But I don't like feeling as if I am an animal on the verge of extinction, so I have settled on 'lesbiana' in Spanish, because I want to honor in my native language my relationships with women. In English, I use the word 'queer.' It's a compromise. Words often are."

—Daisy Hernandez,
writer and editor

2S stands for **two-spirit** or **two-spirited.** This is a term used by some First Nations people to refer to a person who has both a masculine and a feminine spirit. It is sometimes used as a broader term to include same-sex attraction and a wide variety of gender identities and expressions. Many Indigenous peoples have specific terms in their own languages that more accurately describe the social and spiritual roles of gender-variant members of their community. Historically, these individuals were often respected and highly valued.

Q is for **queer,** a term sometimes used by LGBTQ people to refer to all those whose gender identity or sexual orientation falls outside the dominant heterosexual and gender-conforming mainstream. It also carries a political meaning—a challenge to the idea that heterosexuality and traditional gender identities are somehow "normal." People who identify as queer often emphasize the connections between different systems of oppression and the ways in which these systems reinforce each other.

Q can also be for **questioning,** which refers to people who may not currently identify as LGBTQ but are in the process of exploring and discovering their sexual orientation, gender identity or gender expression.

Intersex people are those whose physical sex (their body, their chromosomes and their hormones) doesn't fit easily into traditional categories of male or female.

A stands for **asexual**. People who identify as asexual are generally not sexually attracted to anyone and feel little or no sexual desire.

A also stands for **ally**, someone who supports the rights and freedoms of a marginalized or oppressed group that they aren't a part of themselves. For example, heterosexual high school students often join Gay-Straight Alliances to advocate for greater support and acceptance of LGBTQ students in their schools.

PFLAG: PARENTS AS ALLIES

One group of allies that is very visible in every Pride parade is PFLAG: an organization that provides support for families, allies and people who are LGBTQ, as well as engaging in education and advocacy to bring about full equality. When I came out as a lesbian, my parents started a PFLAG group because they wanted to support the fight for equal rights. My mother, Ilse, remembers: "I first walked in a Pride parade in Toronto in 1992. My daughter

> *"Two-spirited people are said to be gifted twice. We consider them very valuable people."*
> —Trudy Spiller, Gitxsan mother, grandmother and great-grandmother, Victoria, BC

A First Nations marcher wears a traditional button blanket in a Pride parade in Vancouver, BC.
Tony Sprackett

PFLAG members and supporters carrying messages of love and acceptance. Tony Sprackett

had come out the year before and I wanted to support her. I was somewhat unsure how it would be, not being much of a parade kind of person, but it was one of the most overwhelming experiences of my life. As the group of parents walked by, the noise of the crowd watching us grew to a roar: shouts and whistles, and people of all ages rushing up to give us hugs, saying, 'Thank you, thank you!' I had no idea that the support of a group of parents would mean so much."

My mother, Ilse, hands out PFLAG flyers at a Pride parade in Toronto in the mid-1990s. Robin Stevenson

LADIES AND GENTLEMEN, BOYS AND GIRLS…

Our society likes to classify people, and one of the most basic categories that we structure our society around is sex. Male and female. Men and women. Boys and girls.

But it isn't really that simple. There are many more intersex people than you might think. Every year, thousands of babies are born with anatomy or genetics that don't fit neatly into the categories of male or female. For example, a person may be chromosomally male but their physical development may appear more typically female because of an insensitivity to male hormones; or a person may be born with mosaic genetics, so that some of their

My parents, Giles and Ilse, hanging out with my sleepy, face-painted three-year-old at Victoria's Pride Festival in 2007. Robin Stevenson

Amanda Saenz is a fourth-year university student studying philosophy and bioethics in Seattle. They identify as both intersex and non-binary. Amanda works to be an advocate for their community.
Photo by Emily Quinn

"Pride is an opportunity: it creates a space where people come together to not only celebrate the progress made in LGBT+ politics, but also to learn about the histories of the diverse identities that Pride celebrates by creating a safe environment that naturally fosters healthy discussion...Being intersex is something that I have come to accept and cherish about myself. To see so much positivity flying around when people talk about intersexuality only makes me more hopeful for the future because it means that things are getting better."

—Amanda Saenz

cells have XX (female) chromosomes and some of them have XY (male) chromosomes.

Until quite recently, doctors usually assigned a sex to intersex babies—deciding for them whether they would be raised as male or female. Often they operated on babies to make their genitalia conform to the gender they had assigned them. Parents were advised not to tell anyone about their child's condition, and the children themselves were usually kept in the dark about their medical history and the procedures performed on them.

In more recent years, intersex adults have spoken out against these practices and the shame and secrecy that resulted from them. They have organized to work for change, and some have allied themselves with the LGBTQ community. Being intersex is a physical condition, not a sexual orientation or a gender identity, but like gay, lesbian, bisexual and transgender people, intersex people face oppression based on sexism and homophobia. It makes sense to come together to fight for a world in which all those who live outside traditional sex and gender norms can freely express themselves and be proud of who they are.

Sydney Mardi Gras Parade, Australia.
Jeffrey Feng

PROUD MOMENTS

MY COMING-OUT STORY

Me, age twenty-two. Robin Stevenson

I didn't come out as a teenager. I had a few friends who were gay, but I didn't start to question my own sexual orientation until after I graduated from high school, spent a couple of years at university and went to Australia to work. I was twenty-one. I got a job at a university cafeteria and spent lots of time looking after horses and riding along gum-tree-lined trails in the South Australia heat.

I also thought a lot about my past relationships and what I wanted in the future. I broke up with my boyfriend. And I started dating women.

After I returned to Canada, I came out to my parents and my friends. Sometimes I said I was a lesbian. Sometimes I said I was bisexual. Sometimes I identified as queer. I wasn't always sure what language fit best, but one thing I was sure about was that I did not want to hide who I was—or who I loved—from the people that mattered to me.

I was lucky. My parents, my brother and sister, and most of my friends were open-minded and queer-positive individuals who have always supported me completely. Sadly, not everyone is met with the kind of support that I received.

I have friends whose coming out was met with anger, judgment and even rejection from the people they loved.

Coming out is a process that never really ends. More than twenty years later, I still have to come out to people regularly. But why is my sexual orientation anyone's business?

Here's the thing: Being queer isn't just about my sexual orientation—it's about my life! I am coming out when I introduce people to my family. I'm coming out when my partner and I hold hands in public. I'm coming out when I explain that my son doesn't have a dad, he has two mothers. I'm coming out every time I mention my partner by her obviously female name.

Because we live in a culture that tends to assume people are heterosexual unless they say otherwise, heterosexual or "straight" people don't have to come out.

My mother and her friend Irene co-founded PFLAG Hamilton in the early 1990s to provide information and support to other parents of LGBTQ kids, and to advocate for equal rights.
Robin Stevenson

At Toronto's Pride Parade in the early 1990s.
Robin Stevenson

PROUD MOMENTS

COMING OUT IN HIGH SCHOOL

Duncan Smith, playing piano at home in Ontario.
Heather Smith

Duncan Smith is a seventeen-year-old high school student who lives in Ontario. He came out at a much younger age than I did. "I first began questioning my sexuality when I was around twelve or thirteen," he told me. "It was around that age when I started to realize that I was 'different.' However, I didn't 'officially' come out until about fourteen."

Duncan began by talking to one person he trusted. "I started out by telling my closest friend," he says. "That was the first time I openly spoke about my sexuality. It felt good to finally be open about that aspect of myself, so, naturally, I wanted to share with a few more close friends and family members. Next I told my parents, which was probably the hardest thing to do. But it went wonderfully; both were very positive and understanding! It was relieving, but not at all surprising: my parents are both accepting, loving people. That was probably my best experience."

Outside his family, Duncan did encounter some homophobic attitudes. "There were a few less-than-satisfactory reactions from a couple of friends, particularly those with highly religious views," he recalls. "One friend even went so far as to suggest that homosexuality is caused by a 'birth defect.'" Still, he counts himself lucky, as the people who mattered most to him were very supportive.

Duncan says that he isn't a huge fan of labels. "I identify as gay—not for myself, as I am happy to be me; I don't need to be confined within a label," he explains. "I apply this label to my sexuality because it seems to make things easier for others to understand."

The concept of Pride is one he has thought a lot about. "To me, Pride means that you are happy about who you are and feel comfortable in your own skin," he says. "It means that you don't have to hide who you are... I believe that having pride can help you embrace others within your community. When you can accept yourself, you can accept others more easily. That's what Pride is about, for me, at least."

"Pride comes in many different forms; everybody shows their pride in different ways. The expression of pride is just as diverse as the community itself."
—Duncan Smith, age 17, Waterloo, ON

"The pressures on gay teens can be overwhelming—to keep secrets, tell lies, deny who you are, and try to be who you're not. Remember: you are special and worth being cared about, loved and accepted just as you are. Never, ever let anyone convince you otherwise."
—Alex Sanchez, YA author

QUEER FACT

ALTHOUGH MANY LGBTQ TEENS are happy, confident and surrounded by supportive friends and family, others experience significant difficulties in their lives. Compared with heterosexual teens, LGBTQ youth are at increased risk for bullying, harassment, physical assault and other forms of violence—and they are more than twice as likely to attempt suicide. Homelessness is also more common among LGBTQ youth, with family rejection being a major contributing factor.

Schools can promote health and safety among LGBTQ teens by implementing anti-bullying policies, encouraging student-led support groups such as Gay-Straight Alliances, creating safe and welcoming spaces and ensuring access to counselling and resources, and providing training for staff on how to create supportive school environments for all students. Parents, family members and friends of LGBTQ teens can also make a big difference by listening, being accepting and supportive, respecting their choices and their privacy, educating themselves about LGBTQ issues, and publicly supporting equal rights.

PROUD MOMENTS

FIGHTING FOR FAIRNESS

Harriette Cunningham proudly shows her new birth certificate. Sandy Aitken

Twelve-year-old Harriette Cunningham lives with her family on Vancouver Island. When she was born, everyone thought she was a boy—but she never felt like one. As a young child, Harriette wanted to grow her hair long and wear dresses. "I've always known I was a girl, even when I was considered to be a boy," she explained. "In my dreams, I was never a boy."

As Harriette got older, she had to help her parents see who she really was—not their son, but their daughter. Once they understood that she was transgender, they supported her one hundred percent.

Harriette has a strong sense of justice, and it didn't seem fair that even after she changed her name and started living as a girl, her birth certificate still said she was a boy. And it caused practical problems too—whenever she signed up for sports, or traveled to the United States to visit her grandmother, she had to show a document that inevitably caused questions and confusion.

So Harriette, her parents and her grandmother decided they would fight for the right to change her birth certificate to reflect her gender identity. They wrote dozens of letters to British Columbia's government, and when the legislation in the province was finally changed, Harriette was one of the first—and the youngest—in line to get her new birth certificate.

Harriette's birth certificate is a victory, but she isn't done yet. She has filed a human rights complaint to argue gender designation should be removed from birth certificates altogether. "So when a child is born, they won't label it," Harriette said. "If that had happened for me, it would've been a whole lot easier."

> *"Pride is celebrating who you are and being true to who you are."*
> —Harriette Cunningham, Comox, BC

Harriette with her little brother, three-year-old Khosi. Sandy Aitken

At the Pride parade in Milan, Italy, in 2015.
Eugenio Marongiu/Shutterstock.com

3

CELEBRATING PRIDE TODAY

WHAT HAPPENS ON PRIDE DAY?

Pride Day is a celebration of diversity and equality, a day when everyone can express who they truly are. In many places, Pride Day has grown into Pride Week—and that takes a lot of organizing! Many cities have large planning committees that work hard to organize a variety of activities over the week leading up to Pride Day. Every celebration is a little bit different, and each community adds its own flavor to the festivities, but most Pride celebrations include a parade and a festival, and a number of other events.

People of all ages take part in New York City's Pride March. Erika Cross/Shutterstock.com

PRIDE PARADES

The Pride parade is the highlight of most Pride Day celebrations. Pride parades range in size from a few dozen people to hundreds of thousands. Some are relatively quiet and low-key, while others are lavishly extravagant productions. The parades often include floats—gorgeously decorated trucks playing music and loaded with people dancing.

Many groups and organizations march in Pride parades, usually carrying banners to show who they are and what they represent. Some of the groups you might see in a Pride parade include unions, political parties, local businesses, community centers, police forces, food banks, sports organizations, schools and churches.

Others march on their own or with family or friends. A Pride parade can be a very social event, with people

"Pride is a bunch of people getting together to say that they are different and they are okay with that."

—Zea, age 12

Two children carry a Pride flag in Vancouver's Pride Parade. Tony Sprackett

Pride parades and festivals make a fun day out for families and people of all ages. Tony Sprackett

running into acquaintances and stopping to chat along the way. My partner, my son and I usually sit on the sidelines and watch the parade—but we keep jumping up to say hello to friends and walk with them for a stretch. We often see people at Pride whom we haven't seen for months! For many families, Pride is a fun day out.

DRESSING UP FOR PRIDE

For lots of people, a Pride parade is a chance to dress up, to get in touch with their inner performer and to strut their stuff. It's a time to get out the highest heels, the wildest wigs, the longest eyelashes, the brightest feather boas. Of course, the streets are also full of people in T-shirts and shorts—but many pictures of Pride parades show people wearing elaborate, colorful, sometimes over-the-top costumes.

My friends Lindsay, Dea and their toddler Zinnian celebrate Pride as part of a group of queer farmers. They handed out bunches of rainbow chard all along the Pride parade route! Robin Stevenson

Dykes on Bikes lead the way at the start of many Pride parades. Tony Sprackett

When I first came out, I wasn't completely comfortable with this aspect of Pride parades. I was pretty shy and and the last thing I wanted to do was draw attention to myself. I worried that people would see a few pictures of a Pride parade and think that all LGBTQ people wore outrageous costumes all the time: Pink wigs! Sparkly tutus! Fairy wings!

Duncan, the Ontario teenager you met in the last chapter, shared a similar reaction. "I've attended a St. John's Pride Parade in Newfoundland. Personally, I'm not into those sort of events—it's a little too much for me. I find them loud and a bit 'in your face,'" he told me. "As an introverted gay person, I want people to know that being gay does not mean that I am necessarily a flamboyant and over-the-top individual."

Of course, the LGBTQ community is made up of all kinds of people—and no particular image can ever represent us all. For most people, the way they dress in the Pride parade isn't the way they dress every day. That fellow in the sequined dress and high heels, dancing on the float? Probably wears jeans to his day job at the garden center. And the leather-clad woman on the motor bike, with the rainbow-collared rottweiler riding on the back? She looks different in her gray suit when she defends clients in a courtroom.

Dressing up can be a lot of fun, but there is more to it than that. In the first chapter of this book, you read about how LGBTQ people used to be arrested for wearing clothing that crossed traditional gender lines—sometimes called cross-dressing—and you read about the important role drag queens played at Stonewall and throughout LGBTQ history. Today, queer people who don't conform to traditional ideas about gender are more likely to be harassed and even beaten up. Boys who wear makeup and girls who wear suits to the prom often don't have an easy time in school. There is a lot of pressure to fit in. But at Pride, everyone has the space to safely express themselves and wear whatever they like—and celebrate their freedom to do so.

At Pride, people celebrate their freedom to express themselves by dressing however they choose. Some people wear beautiful and elaborate costumes.
Tony Sprackett

Two men walk hand in hand in a Pride parade in Oslo, Norway.
Nanisimova/Shutterstock.com

I still tend to wear my regular clothes to Pride—plus a rainbow flag or two—but these days one of my favorite things about the parade is seeing the incredibly imaginative, artistic and stunningly gorgeous costumes that some people wear. The Pride parade is a showcase of the creative spirit and the diverse beauty of the LGBTQ community—and I am very proud to be a part of it.

THE POLITICS OF PRIDE

Pride Day is a celebration, and sometimes it feels like a great big party…but its roots are strongly political. Coming out and openly living our lives and identifying ourselves as part of the queer community is, in itself, a powerful and political act, and one that has led to a great deal of change. Being visible is important—and thousands of people in a parade are definitely visible!

But the politics of Pride are complicated. The LGBTQ community is a very diverse one, and many people within it experience multiple forms of oppression. For example, a black teenage boy who is coming out as a young gay man faces not just homophobia but also racism. Queer people who have disabilities have to deal with false assumptions, prejudice and discrimination. Racism, sexism, ableism—these are complex systems that intersect and reinforce each other. For Pride to truly represent all LGBTQ people, Pride events need to take a stand against not just homophobia and heterosexism but against all forms of oppression.

In a Pride parade, many people march to bring awareness to a particular issue. If you read the signs and banners being carried by marchers, you will get a glimpse of some of the political battles that are being fought: *Support our*

Maia (top) and Violet celebrating Pride on Salt Spring Island. "I think it is cool to just be yourself. I feel like some people have to give up some friends to have their freedom, but I think it is worth it to be yourself.... And I guess when I go to Pride Parade that's really what I'm supporting." —Maia Jen MacLellan

Pride parades and Pride marches are about political activism as well as celebration. Participants make their communities visible, demand equal rights, and stand up for social justice. Tony Sprackett

A man holds a Pride flag at the 2015 Pride Parade in Rome, Italy. Shutterstock.com

LGBTQ Seniors! Queers Against Racism! Fight Transphobia! People With Disabilities: Also Here, Also Queer!

Community and school-based LGBTQ youth groups are often visible in Pride parades. Queer kids and teens are coming out at younger ages, which in many ways is a good thing—it shows that more young people are accepting themselves and realizing that it is okay to be open about who they are. On the other hand, if their families and peers are not supportive, LGBTQ youth can be at high risk for bullying, rejection and even homelessness. Helping LGBTQ youth who are facing problems at school and at home is an important priority for advocacy groups.

FESTIVALS AND POST-PARADE PARTIES

Pride parade routes are often planned to end at a park, where the parade turns into a great big party often called a Pride festival or post-parade party. Marchers, spectators and the general public are welcome to join in and spend the rest of the day enjoying a Pride festival in a park. Pride festivals usually feature a stage with live music and entertainment, people dancing, food wagons and beer gardens, and vendors selling everything from ice cream to rainbow hats and ties. It's a great time to catch up with friends and soak up the atmosphere.

QUEER FACT

HOMOPHOBIA is the fear or hatred of people who are gay, lesbian or bisexual.

HETEROSEXISM is the system of beliefs and attitudes based on the idea that everyone is or should be attracted to the opposite sex. This system of belief leads to prejudice and discrimination against LGBTQ people.

Pride festivals often include a special kid-friendly zone, with entertainment geared to children and families. In Toronto, Family Pride runs all weekend long, offering snacks, music, games and crafts. San Francisco has an LGBT Family Garden, with a playground and plenty of activities, special LGBTQ Family Days at local museums, and even a Pride Kids Fun Run. The festival my family goes to is much smaller than the ones in bigger cities—but it still has a children's area with bouncy castles, face painting, Hula-Hoops and craft stations.

Most Pride festivals include some activities for kids—like fabulous face painting! Robin Stevenson

OTHER PRIDE WEEK EVENTS

In many cities, Pride Day comes at the end of a week or more of special events. Pride events can include concerts,

I love seeing families celebrating Pride together. As this dad's T-shirt says: Respect the right to be different. Robin Stevenson

Puppy Pride! This handsome fellow is enjoying the sunshine and the sea breeze at Victoria's annual Big Gay Dog Walk. Robin Stevenson

In Stuttgart, Germany, waiting for the start of the Christopher Street Day Parade. AMzPhoto/iStock.com

drag shows, sporting events, film festivals, theatrical productions, nightclub parties, Pride Idol and more.

As a writer and book lover, one of my favorite events every year is a literary one. Pride in the Word is an evening featuring readings from LGBTQ poets and writers. There really is something for everyone. Victoria's Pride Week even has an event for queer dog owners: The Big Gay Dog Walk!

SYMBOLS OF PRIDE: RAINBOW FLAGS AND PINK TRIANGLES

If you go to a Pride parade or a Pride festival, you will see a lot of rainbows.

Why all the rainbows? It goes back to 1978, when artist and activist Gilbert Baker designed a rainbow flag as a symbol of pride and diversity, and flew it at San Francisco's

Thousands of revelers participate in Pride Istanbul, showing off a multitude of colorful flags. Sami Sert/iStock.com

Each year in June, San Francisco's City Hall is lit with rainbow colors in celebration of Pride.
Nickolay Stanev/Shutterstock.com

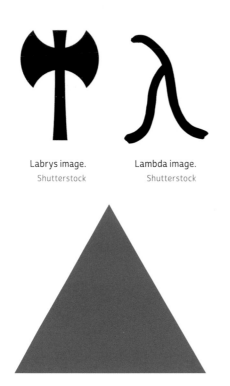

Labrys image.
Shutterstock

Lambda image.
Shutterstock

Pride Day. Another symbol that you might notice on T-shirts, signs and banners is the pink triangle. Its origin is a disturbing one: In the concentration camps of Nazi Germany during the Second World War, all prisoners were forced to wear a badge identifying them. Jews wore the yellow star. Gay men wore the pink triangle. Thousands of gay men were imprisoned in Nazi concentration camps and many of them died. In the 1970s, the gay community reclaimed the pink triangle, originally intended as a badge of shame, and turned it into a symbol of Pride.

Other symbols you might see at a Pride event include the *labrys*—a double-headed ax from ancient Crete, which represents lesbian and feminist strength—and the *lambda*—a Greek letter used in many countries as a symbol of gay and lesbian community. The lambda was adopted as the international symbol for gay and lesbian rights by the International Gay Rights Congress in Scotland in 1974. The Lambda Literary Awards (affectionately known as the Lammies) are given out each year to recognize and honor the best new LGBTQ books and writers. The lambda and the labrys aren't as visible as all the rainbow flags—but if you look for them at a Pride festival, you'll probably find a few! They are often used on signs, T-shirts and jewelry. You might also see a pink equal sign—a popular symbol for marriage equality.

QUEER FACT

THE RAINBOW FLAG, OR PRIDE FLAG, originally had eight colors, but pink and turquoise have since been dropped—because pink fabric was hard to find! The Pride flag now has six horizontal stripes: red, orange, yellow, green, blue and violet.

PERFORMING GENDER: DRAG QUEENS AND DRAG KINGS

Many Pride parades and festivals include drag shows—performances by drag queens or drag kings. Drag queens are generally men who dress in an exaggeratedly feminine fashion, with heavy makeup, glamorous dresses and high heels. Drag kings are women who dress as men or perform typically male roles—for example, doing a stage show lip-synching songs by male singers. For most drag queens and kings, drag is about performance and creative expression. It is hard to generalize when it comes to drag performers and drag culture, because there are many different kinds of drag, but one thing is for sure: drag has been a part of

It's drag queens versus drag kings in Victoria Pride's annual drag ball game. In 2015, Mayor Lisa Helps donned a mustache and joined the game!
Victoria Pride Society/PBJ Photography

"Anyone can wear a dress—male, female, or anyone in between! I am a guy. I love performing as female characters on the stage in front of crowds of people. Doing drag allows me to become any character I can imagine! Drag allows me to bring some extra sparkle and smiles to my and other people's lives and that's why I do it. I do drag because I love how it makes me and others feel!" —Ryan, AKA Dixie Paul Chappel

A family participates in the San Francisco
Pride Parade. kobbydagan /iStock.com

gay culture in western countries for a very long time, and
Pride wouldn't be the same without it.

FAMILY PRIDE

For many families, Pride Day is an important annual celebration. The first time I took my son to Pride Day, in 2004,
he was one month old—and, of course, he slept through
most of it! We have been every year since then. As a parent,
one of the things I like about Pride is that my son gets to
see that families come in an infinite variety of configura-
tions—that there are many different kinds of families to
celebrate. There are single-parent families. There are families with two moms and families with two dads. There
are blended families, families with step-parents, families

formed through divorce and remarriage. There are families with transgender parents. Some families are formed through adoption. Some gay men create families with the help of a surrogate mother. Some lesbians conceive with the help of sperm donors.

And, of course, you don't have to have kids to be a family. Some LGBTQ people consider their closest friends to be another kind of family—a family of choice.

At Pride, it's okay to be all of who you are. One of the songs that is often played at North American Pride festivals is "We Are Family"—and at Pride, that's usually how I feel.

Muslims for Progressive Values supporting LGBTQ rights in a Pride parade in Columbus, Ohio.
Picklesaddie /Dreamstime.com

PRIDE AND RELIGION

Of course, your sexual orientation is only one part of who you are. We all have many different aspects to our identities,

St. John the Divine Church showing support for the LGBTQ community at Victoria's Pride Parade.
Tony Sprackett

In Copenhagen, Denmark, Jewish marchers carry a rainbow flag with the Star of David on it. Flemming Hansen/iStock.com

Quoting Pope Francis, Catholics march in support of Pride. Tony Sprackett

and for a lot of people, one important part of who they are is their religion. Jewish, Protestant, Muslim, Catholic, Hindu, Wiccan, Buddhist…there are LGBTQ people within every religious tradition.

Historically, much opposition to LGBTQ rights has come from religious organizations, and for LGBTQ people who have a strong religious identity, this conflict often causes emotional pain and self-doubt. It can make coming out more difficult and can lead to difficulties with family members. In some cases, coming out leads to rejection by one's religious community.

And yet, within every religious tradition, there are strong voices calling for acceptance, for equality, for change. More and more religious organizations are welcoming LGBTQ people and standing up for equality,

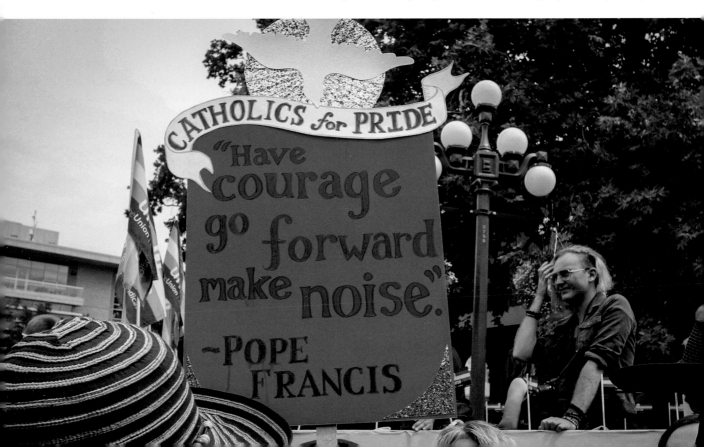

CATHOLICS for PRIDE
"Have courage go forward make noise."
-POPE FRANCIS

and some religious groups now recognize same-sex marriages. Many churches, synagogues and faith groups, as well as some Muslim organizations, show their support of LGBTQ people by participating in Pride parades and festivals.

The group Universalist Muslims, which describes itself as "queer affirming," works for human rights and has a visible presence in Pride parades. Shahla Khan Salter, one of the founders of Universalist Muslims, says, "We think it's very important to spread that message that we are all equal and we stand shoulder to shoulder with our queer Muslim [family] and our queer friends of other faiths as well. We actually believe that it is contrary to Islam to persecute sexual minorities."

"I felt deeply grateful to be part of something where I felt like I was letting people know in a very public way that they were loved," said Rabbi Shoshanah Conover of Temple Sholom, about marching in Chicago's Pride Parade. "It felt good to me that collectively here we are in this huge parade, all of us together, to show this openness and welcoming. It was truly pride."

A huge rainbow flag flies from the Westerkerk Protestant Church in Amsterdam, the Netherlands. The sky is filled with pink confetti from a passing boat in Amsterdam's famous Canal Parade. digitalimagination/iStock.com

CONTROVERSY, CHALLENGE AND CHANGE

In recent years, the LGBTQ community has made huge progress. Here in Canada, our legal rights are protected, and same-sex relationships are increasingly accepted. There are still battles to be fought, but we can also celebrate the fact that our families are able to live more openly and safely than at any time in history.

> *"Pride is a time to celebrate the diversity, resilience and beauty of the queer community."*
> —Amanda Littauer, author, historian, mother

Forty-five years after the Stonewall Riots, an estimated two million people attended the 2015 Pride March in New York City.
Kobby Dagan/Shutterstock.com

As LGBTQ people became more visible, politicians began attending Pride parades to show support—and seek votes. Businesses recognized that Pride Day was an opportunity for them to promote their products and services. Banks, taxi and tourism companies, restaurants, bars and nightclubs all began decorating floats and joining the parades. While being seen as potential customers is certainly an improvement over being refused service, many in the LGBTQ community dislike the increasing commercialization and consumerism of Pride Day celebrations.

Others feel that Pride events don't represent them. Transgender people, people of color, people with disabilities, two-spirited people and others have argued that their

There are always lots of smiling faces at Pride! For me, it is a joyful and very moving experience to see so many people celebrating the diversity of our LGBTQ communities and feeling safe to express their identities and their love. Tony Sprackett

Eleven-year-old Zoë watches the Chicago Pride Parade from a balcony with her two moms, Amanda and Laura, and her one-year-old sister, Lilah. Brian Sandberg

Toronto Dyke March. mikecphoto/Shutterstock.com

New York City's Dyke March—not a parade, but a protest against discrimination, harassment and violence. a katz/Shutterstock.com

lives and identities are marginalized within the LGBTQ community and within Pride celebrations. Pride parades tend to be so dominated by white, cisgender, able-bodied gay men that other identities become invisible.

Many large cities hold dyke marches as part of Pride Week. Dyke marches are not parades—they are political demonstrations organized to increase visibility for lesbians and transgender people and all women who love women, however they identify themselves. In the last few years, trans marches have also become part of many pride celebrations, with the goal of increasing visibility, awareness and acceptance of transgender people.

Last year, I attended an Alt Pride march in Victoria. Alt Pride—or Alternative Pride—is a grassroots political

event that strives to challenge racism, colonialism and transphobia, to embrace the full diversity of LGBTQ people by making transgendered, two-spirited and other marginalized identities more visible, and to provide a non-commercial alternative to Pride. In Victoria, a group of activists gathered at a local community center to make signs and then marched to a nearby park for drumming, music, food and socializing.

Dyke marches, trans marches and alternative Pride marches are often wonderful events, celebrating some of the many identities and communities that make up the larger queer community, but it is important to recognize why they have become necessary and to work toward making *all* Pride events more inclusive.

My local neighborhood community center hosts a sign-making workshop for those who want to take part in the Alt Pride March. Robin Stevenson

One of my friends made rainbow cookies to hand out to people taking part in the Alt Pride March. Robin Stevenson

PROUD MOMENTS

ISLAND PRIDE

I met Zea and her moms, Wendy (left) and Cory, at Victoria's Pride celebrations.
Robin Stevenson

Meet twelve-year-old Zea Martin-Hanson and her family: her two moms, Wendy and Cory; her dad, Steve; and her older sister, Jazz.

Zea and her family live on Protection Island, which is a very special place: a tiny island off the coast of a larger island. It is located near the city of Nanaimo, on Vancouver Island's east coast. There is no bridge to the island, and with only three hundred residents, Zea and her family consider everyone who lives on Protection Island to be their neighbors.

For more than ten years, their family celebrated Pride Day in Vancouver, Victoria and Nanaimo. It was an important day for them. Wendy explains, "Pride shows my kids how many other gay people are out there, that being different is wonderful and fun, and that their family is just another kind of family—and one that is worth celebrating."

In the last few years, though, Wendy has been ill, and traveling to the city for Pride has been more difficult. So, two years ago, the family organized their own small Pride Day celebration—a potluck dinner with the queer people that they knew on Protection Island. "There were five couples at this event," Wendy recalls. "Zea found it really boring—no other kids and just adults talking!"

This past summer, they decided to try ramping it up a bit—and organized a parade! "The community really got into it," Wendy says. "Lots of people got dressed up with rainbow face paint and rainbow clothes. There were probably eighty to a hundred people participating and others watching from the sides." Not a bad turnout for an island whose entire population is only three hundred!

Most people on Protection Island don't have cars, so the parade had golf carts instead of floats. It also had lots of decorated bikes, because Zea had organized the island's kids to decorate them together. And after the parade was over, they all went to the park on the beach and hung out. "Many of us went swimming, as it was a gorgeous day," Wendy says. "It was a fantastic experience and we are planning to make it an annual event. It was different than other Pride parades we've been a part of as the majority of participants were straight!"

"This event added to my experience of Pride," Zea's mom Cory adds. "I could feel my friends' and neighbors' pride in me and my family and other queer neighbors."

Twelve-year-old Zea, with some of the bikes she helped decorate for Protection Island's Pride parade. Robin Stevenson

Island residents drive golf carts in Protection Island's first Pride parade. Robin Stevenson

A crowd gathers in front of the Coliseum during a Pride parade in Rome, Italy.
alessandro0770/iStock.com

4

PRIDE AROUND THE WORLD

FIGHTING FOR FREEDOM AND EQUALITY

For many people, Pride is a celebration—but it is important not to let the rainbows and parades mask the ongoing struggles that LGBTQ people still face. There is no federal law protecting LGBTQ people from discrimination in the United States, and in more than half the states, people can still be fired for their sexual orientation. Transgender people have even less protection— in more than thirty states, it is legal to fire someone solely because they are transgender. Queer teens continue to be kicked out of their homes. Transgender people and queer people of color face horrifying rates of violence, hate crimes and murder.

At the London, UK, Pride Parade, a marcher lifts a sign demanding trans rights. In England, North America and around the world, trans people continue to face harassment, discrimination and violence.
Bikeworldtravel/Shutterstock.com

And in some parts of the world, LGBTQ people are still fighting for the most basic of rights—the right to be who they are without fear of violence or imprisonment.

In many countries, being openly gay or lesbian may mean facing persecution, imprisonment and even death. According to a 2015 report, same-sex relationships are still illegal in seventy-five countries—and in five of those countries (Iran, Saudi Arabia, Mauritania, Sudan and Yemen) individuals in such relationships can be punished with the death penalty.

While some countries are moving toward equality, others seem to be slipping further and further away from it. Same-sex relationships are illegal in thirty-seven of Africa's fifty-four countries—and in the last few years, a number of those countries have introduced harsh new anti-gay laws. African anti-gay legislation is one of the legacies of colonialism—many traditional cultures were in fact tolerant of diverse sexualities and gender identities.

In Eastern Europe, where same-sex relationships are not against the law, several countries have introduced or are considering laws that limit free speech by banning what they call "gay propaganda"—which includes all Pride celebrations, as well as any efforts to protect or promote LGBTQ rights.

Despite these risks, LGBTQ people around the world continue to fight for their rights. As Duncan Smith, the teen whose coming-out story you read in Chapter Two, says, "LGBT equality is when everybody, regardless of their sexual or gender identity, is treated as equal. This is not achieved until everybody on our planet Earth can feel safe about expressing their sexual orientation."

US Consular Services in Toronto, ON, ready for World Pride. Stacie DaPonte/Wikipedia

GOING GLOBAL: WORLD PRIDE

In 2014, World Pride was held in Toronto, ON. **Above** mikecphoto/Shutterstock.com, **and below** Stacie DaPonte/Wikipedia

World Pride, as its name suggests, is an international celebration of LGBTQ Pride. It is organized by InterPride, an organization that is made up of Pride co-ordinators from around the world. InterPride chooses the city where World Pride events will be held, and selects a theme for that year's festivities. World Pride festivals, which are usually several years apart, include at least a week of art, sports and social events leading up to the World Pride Parade. Rome hosted the first World Pride event in 2000, followed by Jerusalem and London.

In 2014, World Pride was held in North America for the first time, and the host city was Toronto, Ontario. The theme for this fourth World Pride was "Rise Up," and the Canadian

World Pride Toronto, 2014. Stacie DaPonte/Wikipedia

band Parachute Club released a new remix of its iconic song "Rise Up" just in time for the ten-day-long celebration. Events included an international human rights conference, an exhibition marking the forty-fifth anniversary of Stonewall, and ten open-air stages featuring performances by numerous musicians and artists. The weekend-long street fair featured a kid-friendly Family Pride space, with activities and entertainment geared to children and families.

Toronto's World Pride also included three marches—the Trans March, the Dyke March and the World Pride Parade. All were well-attended, with the World Pride Parade setting a record for length: it lasted over five hours! Over two hundred elaborately decorated floats took part, thousands of people marched, and many tens of thousands more watched the parade.

Toronto buses and crosswalks were painted with rainbow stripes, the CN Tower was lit up with rainbow lights, and Niagara Falls shone with the colors of Pride. And over a hundred same-sex couples—some of whom traveled from other countries, including Australia, Scotland and Taiwan—tied the knot in a Grand Pride Wedding!

The next World Pride will be held in 2017 in Madrid, Spain.

EUROPE

Many European countries celebrate Pride with parades, film festivals, concerts and other events. Austria's capital city, Vienna, decorates all of its trams with rainbow flags for the month leading up to its Pride parade. Germany boasts huge parades in both Cologne and Berlin, as well

At a Pride parade in Viareggio, a small city in northern Tuscany, Italy. Lucky Team Studio/ Shutterstock.com

The Pride parade in Rome, Italy, draws many thousands of people. Lucky Team Studio/ Shutterstock.com

In Amsterdam, the Pride parade takes place in the city's canals—on floats that actually float!
Freek Frederix/Shutterstock.com

Celebrating Black Pride UK in London, England.
Bikeworldtravel/Shutterstock

London Pride. Manyukhina/Dreamstime.com

as many smaller ones across the country, and France has Pride parades in at least twenty different cities. The United Kingdom holds several large Pride events, with the biggest being in London and Brighton. London also hosts Black Pride UK, to celebrate and promote unity among LGBTQ people of African, Asian, Caribbean, Middle Eastern and Latin American descent. And Amsterdam hosts Canal Pride—a Pride parade held on boats in the city's canals.

In Eastern Europe, the social climate and laws are less supportive of Pride. Some Eastern European countries have not yet held Pride events, and in others, Pride parades have been marked by violent protests, clashes between marchers and anti-gay protestors, injuries and arrests.

EUROPRIDE

EuroPride is Europe's annual Pride celebration, and it has a longer history than World Pride. It began in 1992 and is an annual event hosted by a different European city each year. EuroPride has been held in many spectacular locations, including Berlin, Stockholm, London, Warsaw, Copenhagen, Rome, Marseille, Vienna, Amsterdam, Zurich and Madrid.

Madrid, the capital of Spain, hosted EuroPride in 2007—and set a record for the biggest Pride celebration ever. An incredible two and a half million people attended. The Spanish LGBTQ community had reason to celebrate— their government had recently changed laws to allow same-sex marriage and adoption.

When World Pride is held in Europe, it counts as EuroPride as well—so Madrid's World Pride 2017 will also be its second time hosting EuroPride. On top of that, Madrid will be celebrating the fortieth anniversary of Spain's first Pride parade, back in 1977. Sounds like Madrid is the place to be in 2017!

A huge crowd gathers in front of the Metropolis Building during the EuroPride Parade in Madrid, Spain. Oscar San Jose/Wikipedia

QUEER FACT

A VERY INTERNATIONAL EVENT took place in Sweden during Stockholm's Pride festival in 2014: a wedding blessing performed for two Iranian women by an Algerian-born Imam who grew up in France and now lives in South Africa! The two Muslim women, Sahar Mosleh and Maryam Iranfar, may be the first Iranian women to marry each other in a religious ceremony. They now live in Sweden, because in Iran their relationship could be punished by lashings or the death penalty. "I'm glad that this is a happy couple who can now form a family after many years of struggle," said Imam Zahed, who is also gay. Sahar and Maryam, who were legally married in a Swedish civil ceremony four years ago, were expecting their first child at the time of their wedding.

TURKEY

In 2003, Turkey became the first Muslim majority country to hold a Pride parade. Called Gay Pride Istanbul, it was a small event, with about thirty people taking part. However, it was the start of something huge. Every year, more people have attended, and by 2011 the Pride events in Turkey's capital city, Istanbul, attracted over ten thousand people—making it the biggest Pride march in Eastern Europe. Three years later it was ten times bigger again, with over a hundred thousand people. Smaller Pride parades were also held in the Turkish cities of Izmir and Antalya.

Istanbul's Pride march begins in Taksim Square. Participants march the entire length of İstiklal (Independence) Avenue, one of the city's most famous

People celebrate Pride in Istanbul's Taksim Square. After years of peaceful Pride celebrations, Istanbul's Pride March in 2015 was interrupted by police who used rubber bullets and water cannons to disperse the crowds. EvrenKalinbacak/Shutterstock.com

streets. İstiklal Avenue is a wide pedestrian boulevard lined with shops, cafes, art galleries, restaurants, cinemas, churches, synagogues, mosques and embassies. Many of Istanbul's festivals take place here.

While same-sex relationships have never been criminalized in Turkey, the government has failed to take action to protect LGBTQ people. Intolerance and social disapproval are widespread, and hate crimes are common. Many LGBTQ people in Turkey are forced to hide their sexual orientation to avoid harassment, discrimination or violence. Marchers in the Pride parade carried signs calling for change: *Love knows no gender*, *Another kind of family is possible* and *Stop homophobia*. "In Turkey, we all have difficulty exercising our rights," marcher Aykut Yanak told a reporter. "This is why we must fight and why we all walk together today." Another participant, Senef Cakmak, spoke of the personal meaning the event holds: "Today is the only time of year that I am myself. I don't have to hide from anyone."

AUSTRALIA

Australia's largest and most famous Pride festival is the month-long Sydney Mardi Gras, which attracts hundreds of thousands of people from all around the world. It takes place in February and March—summertime in Australia—and includes a parade, numerous parties, concerts and performances, a queer film festival, art shows and a number of sports events, from runs to cycling tours to bowling nights. For families, Victoria Park is a great place to go for Fair Day, with international food, market stalls,

A child rides a scooter in the Sydney Mardi Gras Parade. Jeffrey Feng

"I think a few years from now we're going to look back and wonder how homophobia was ever acceptable."

—Imran Khan, actor

Children clap and dance during the Sydney Mardi Gras Parade in 2015. Over two hundred kids from LGBTI families took part, marching and celebrating with their parents and friends. Hamid Mousa

rides, comedy, dance, live music—and even the famous DoggyWood dog show!

All these events lead up to the Sydney Mardi Gras Parade. The parade is both a celebration and a political demand for LGBTQ rights—including same-sex marriage, which is still not recognized under Australian law. About ten thousand people take part, many riding on fantastic floats or dressed in elaborate costumes. Fireworks are launched from the rooftops of buildings along the parade route, and hundreds of thousands of spectators line the streets to cheer and show their support as the parade goes by.

SOUTH AMERICA

From São Paulo, Brazil, to small towns along the Amazon River, South America is home to some of the world's largest Pride celebrations, as well as some of its most remote ones.

In São Paulo, the entire month of June is Pride Month, and people come from all over the world to celebrate. With same-sex marriage being recognized in 2013, the locals have lots to celebrate too. Brazil's neighbor, Argentina, is also supportive of LGBTQ rights and hosts Pride events that attract many thousands of people.

Also in Brazil, but at the other end of the scale in terms of size, is the small Amazon town of Benjamin Constant, which held its first Pride celebration in 2011. Benjamin Constant is located right at a three-way border with Colombia and Peru, where the Amazon and Javari Rivers intersect. A town of about thirty thousand people, it has a diverse and religious community, little wealth, but abundant local fruit and fish. Benjamin Constant's first Pride celebration included a day-long forum discussing LGBT education, health and security issues, followed by a parade with more than sixty people marching through town, carrying a large rainbow flag. The song "I Will Survive" was played, and a supportive crowd followed along, dancing or riding motorbikes, chanting slogans and honking horns as they made their way down to the port.

Other South American countries, like Peru, have lagged behind when it comes to LGBTQ rights, with discrimination and prejudice being common and same-sex marriage

A big smile on the face of this young marcher in the Sydney Mardi Gras Parade! Hamid Mousa

Supporters hold a banner in Iquitos, Peru: *Regional March Against Transphobia.* Gart van Gennip

not yet being recognized. Lima, Peru, hosts a smaller Pride event. Its claim to fame is that it is run by what is possibly the oldest LGBT rights organization in Latin America; the *Movimiento Homosexual de Lima* (Homosexual Movement of Lima) was established in 1982.

In the meantime, Peruvians continue to celebrate Pride. Iquitos, an isolated jungle town in the Peruvian rain forest that is inaccessible by road, holds an annual Pride parade. "Even in the poorest neighborhoods, people are completely accepted members of the community, and they are able to live the way they want, without fear," one resident told me. About two hundred people take part in the Iquitos Pride Parade, either marching or watching the festivities.

Pride supporters hold a sign in Iquitos: *Homosexuality is not a disease. Homophobia is.* Gart van Gennip

UGANDA

Being gay is still a criminal offense in many African countries. In Uganda, the subject was considered taboo until 2009, when a group of American evangelical preachers went to Uganda to attend an anti-gay conference and helped politicians there draft anti-gay legislation. Originally, the bill proposed the death penalty for people involved in same-sex relationships, but this was later reduced to life imprisonment. Under this law, people could go to jail for fourteen years just for knowing someone who was gay and not reporting them to the police.

The public debate about this law provoked anti-gay feelings in an already conservative country. In 2010, a tabloid newspaper called for gays to be executed. It published a list of a hundred names, photographs and

Uganda's first Pride parade: Cars blasted music; marchers danced, chanted and sang; and children who lived nearby joined in. Rachel Adams

"People chanted at the parade: We are here! We are here!...
We were telling ourselves that despite the guns that they have pointed square in our chests we are still here, standing, fighting, not moved by the storm."
–Cleo, Ugandan transwoman

home addresses of individuals they believed to be gay or lesbian, under the headline *Hang Them*. Three of those individuals—activists David Kato, Kasha Nabagesera and Pepe Julian Onziema—sued the newspaper and won. A few weeks later, David Kato was murdered in his home.

But Uganda's gay and lesbian activists did not give up. Despite the dangers, Kasha Nabagesera and Pepe Julian Onziema continued to fight for LGBTQ rights, and both have received international awards for their human rights advocacy.

In 2012, Uganda held its first Pride celebration. More than fifty people gathered for Uganda Beach Pride in a public park on the banks of Lake Victoria in Entebbe, thirty-five kilometers from the capital city, Kampala. Despite police harassment and several arrests, the event was considered by the LGBTQ community to be a success.

The anti-gay bill was signed into law in February 2014. Gay men and lesbians lost their jobs, were evicted from their apartments and faced increasing violence. A few months later, the law was ruled invalid in court—and shortly after that, Ugandans celebrated their third Pride event. This time, more than two hundred people took part.

The fight for basic human rights is far from over—the government of Uganda has announced its intention to appeal to the Supreme Court to support its anti-gay law. In spite of the dangers, Ugandan activists continue to work to educate the public and pave the way for change.

RUSSIA

Russian LGBTQ activists have been fighting to hold Pride parades for the last ten years, but the Russian government has repeatedly banned these events. The European Court of Human Rights has fined Russia for human rights violations; however, the Russian government paid the fine and went right on banning Pride events. In 2012, a district court in Moscow issued a ruling banning Pride events... for the next hundred years!

"This event for me was about celebrating who I am—a transgender person together with my family. I was celebrating courage, strength and solidarity."
—Pepe Julian Onziema, Ugandan LGBT activist, transman, Stonewall Hero of the Year 2014

Marchers chanted "we are here!"—standing up to government officials who had denied that there were gay people in their country. Rachel Adams

QUEER FACT

SOUTH AFRICA IS THE ONLY COUNTRY on the African continent to have legalized same-sex marriage, and it was the first African country to hold a Pride parade. The first South African Pride parade was held in Johannesburg on October 13, 1990, and events are held annually in a number of locations.

Despite these bans, activists have organized Pride parades every year since 2006. These have been held in May, to commemorate the date on which same-sex relationships ceased to be considered a crime in Russia. Each year, Russian LGBTQ protestors and supporters from across Europe have marched, and each year, they have been attacked by hundreds of anti-gay protestors, who chant homophobic slogans, throw things and even beat and kick participants. Many protestors have been injured by anti-gay extremists, but instead of protecting the marchers, the police have arrested them for participating in the rally.

One of the reasons that activists have been so determined to hold Pride parades is that it leads to media coverage and makes the LGBTQ community more visible. And visibility is key to increasing awareness and changing attitudes.

Russian activists protest their government's homophobic and oppressive anti-gay laws.
Svetlana Moshkova

Every year, LGBTQ people celebrate Pride in Russia despite the risks of doing so. Svetlana Moshkova

In 2013, the Russian government passed a new law that directly attacked this strategy of visibility, making it more difficult—and more dangerous—for LGBTQ activists to fight for their rights. The law banned "propaganda of non-traditional relationships" and was so broadly worded that any public displays of LGBTQ symbols or culture—like holding a rainbow flag—could be considered a crime. This new law could be used to arrest LGBTQ activists and protestors.

Because Russia had been chosen to host the 2014 Olympics in Sochi, the government's oppression of LGBTQ people became the focus of international attention. Athletes, public figures and politicians around the world denounced the country's anti-gay laws. Some called for a boycott. Many athletes—like Canadian speed skater Anastasia Bucsis, Finnish swimmer Ari-Pekka Liukkonen, and Australian

A community worker holds a protest sign: *Rainbow flag against fascism!* Svetlana Moshkova

Russia's LGBTQ community continues to fight for freedom and equality despite the persecution by police and government. In 2015, Nicolai Alexeyev was arrested and jailed for organizing a Pride parade. Svetlana Moshkova

"Today we gathered here, on Marsovo Pole—so brave, so diverse, so beautiful. And many more brave and beautiful people join actions all over Russia to show that we exist and that we are not afraid."

–Svetlana Zakharov, Russian LGBT Network, speaking about IDAHO 2015 (International Day Against Homophobia, Transphobia and Biphobia)

snowboarder Belle Brockhoff—came out publicly as gay or lesbian to lend their support to the chorus of voices raised in protest. Across Canada, dozens of government buildings flew rainbow flags during the Olympic Games to show support for the rights of LGBTQ people in Russia.

Despite the protests, the Sochi games went ahead—and fourteen Russian LGBTQ activists were arrested on the opening day alone. Their so-called crimes? Ten of them waved rainbow flags in Moscow's Red Square. The other four held up a sign quoting the Olympic Charter's ban on any form of discrimination.

Russia's government continues to ban Pride events—and despite the risk of arrest, Russia's LGBTQ community continues to fight for change and celebrate their pride.

KOREA

Korea hosts an annual Pride parade that is one of the largest in Asia. Samuel Murray, a US citizen who had been living in South Korea for two years when he attended his first Pride Day in 2014, gave me an insider account of the event. "Fourteen years ago it was a group of fifty people marching through Seoul with bags over their heads to protect their identities," he told me, "and this year it was a crowd of over twenty thousand."

Despite these numbers, the LGBTQ community in Korea is much less visible than it is in North America and Europe. "Many Koreans believe that homosexuality doesn't exist in their country," Samuel explained. "A lot of gay people stay closeted here for their entire lives...Because Korea is culturally conservative and lacks anti-discrimination laws for

> *"This was my first Pride parade. I waited until I was 25 to come out as bisexual. I had always known that I was attracted to men, but I always ended up dating women, until the burden of presumed straightness was too much to bear."*
> —Samuel Murray

It is illegal to have a camera at Korea's Pride parade without a press pass. Luckily, Samuel had one! Samuel Murray

A rainbow flag flies above the crowds on Pride Day in Seoul, South Korea. Samuel Murray

sexual minorities, being out can entail a lifetime of severe social and professional repercussions."

The 2014 Pride Parade was brought to a standstill when Christian protestors lay in the streets to block the parade route. The marchers refused to give up. They stayed in the streets, kept blasting their music and kept on dancing on top of the parade floats—for five hours! A huge white and red banner reading *Love conquers Hate* flew above the heads of the crowd. Finally, determined to finish the parade, the leaders took the parade on an unplanned route that avoided the protestors. "A crowd of thousands followed," Samuel said, recalling the profound sense of victory.

Change is happening in South Korea, and Pride Day is helping to fuel that change. "Pride needs to exist for the sake of LGBTQ visibility," Samuel said. This visibility is key

Two gay men at a Pride parade in Seoul, South Korea. Samuel Murray

to social change. Because most LGBTQ people in Korea are not out, many Koreans do not know that there are LGBTQ people in their families and among their friends and colleagues. Once they realize this, they may be more inclined toward acceptance and support.

A visible LGBTQ community is also important for young LGBTQ people and those who are in the process of coming out. Samuel observes that many newly out gay men feel pressure to fit into a certain image of gay men that they see in the media, "even if it isn't who they naturally are." In Korea—as elsewhere around the world—Pride parades challenge stereotypes. "They show diversity within the LGBTQ community," Samuel explained. "Pride illustrates that our sexuality isn't the entirety of our identities; it's only one small facet of our complex human makeup."

Pride March in New York City's Greenwich Village.
a katz/Shutterstock.com

INTERNATIONAL ACTIVISM

These days, the global LGBTQ community and its allies are taking full advantage of the possibilities provided by the Internet and social media. From Twitter to Facebook, from Tumblr to Reddit, people come together to talk about what is happening where they live. They share photographs and news articles, and express—and sometimes argue about—their views. They make connections with others and strategize together. All around the world, letter-writing campaigns build and petitions circulate, challenging discrimination and demanding equality.

Money is raised for legal challenges, for public education, for support. Even in the countries with the most oppressive laws, activists make use of the Internet to work for change.

If you want to work toward human rights around the world, you need to know something about the laws that affect LGBTQ citizens. The International Lesbian, Gay, Bisexual, Trans and Intersex Association (ILGA)—a worldwide federation with more than a thousand member organizations, representing over a hundred countries—helps with that. It publishes the annual *State-Sponsored Homophobia Report*, pulling together the latest research and providing activists, as well as lawyers, judges, journalists and others, with accurate and up-to-date information about the current situation in each country. This report has become an important tool in defending human rights, and you can download it online for free. ILGA also produces a world map of LGBTI rights.

In 2011, the United Nations launched the Free and Equal Campaign—its first global public education campaign to counter homophobia and transphobia, and fight for legal reforms and equality. Other organizations, like Amnesty International, draw attention to human rights abuses against LGBTQ people.

An activist carries a sign demanding civil rights in a Pride parade in Bangalore. Same-sex relationships are criminalized in India, and LGBTQ people have no legal protection from discrimination. Despite this, a number of Indian cities host large and vibrant Pride parades.
Jedraszak/iStock.com

Marchers from all over the world are visible in New York City's Pride March, and many carry signs drawing attention to the need for global activism.
isogood/iStock.com

PROUD MOMENTS

Kasha Nabagesera. Martin Ennals Foundation

KASHA NABAGESERA

Growing up as a lesbian in Uganda has meant a lifetime of fighting for Kasha Nabagesera. From the age of seven, she was beaten with a cane for writing love letters to other girls, expelled from numerous schools and forbidden from wearing clothing considered to be more suitable for boys. At her university, a Wanted poster showed her name and photograph, suggesting she was a criminal. Each class of new students was warned that they could be expelled for associating with her. Kasha was not allowed to live on campus and was forced to sign an agreement that she would not go within 100 meters of the girls' hostel.

Despite this brutal treatment, Kasha has always lived openly as a lesbian. The subject was so taboo that for a long time she didn't know that same-sex relationships were illegal. "Every time I got picked on or punished for being a lesbian, I thought they were just using it as an excuse to bully me," she explained. "It's only when I was suspended at university that I took interest in finding out why my sexuality was a big deal for others, and that's when I found out that it was actually illegal to be gay. I did research and found out not only in Uganda and other parts of Africa, but all over the world, and that was my turning point."

In 2003, Kasha founded an LGBTI rights organization called Freedom and Roam Uganda and went on to lead it for the next ten years. Although she was already an accountant, she decided to study human rights law—and began training activists in Uganda and many other African countries. Kasha fought against Uganda's oppressive laws and spoke at numerous international events, raising global awareness of the persecution of Uganda's LGBTI people. She risked her own life by appearing on national television in Uganda, becoming one of the first gay people to openly speak out, and in 2015 she helped launch Uganda's first LGBTI magazine, Bombastic.

Kasha has received numerous international awards and honors for her human rights work. In 2011, she became the first LGBTI activist to be awarded the Martin Ennals Award for Human Rights Defenders. Michelle Kagari of Amnesty International said, "Her passion to promote equality and her tireless work to end a despicable climate of fear is an inspiration to LGBT activists the world over."

> "Pride is a protest and a celebration to me.
> A protest to bring attention to the plight of the many challenges faced by the LGBTQIA community, and to bring about visibility.
> And a celebration for the milestones and achievements registered during the struggle for LGBTQIA freedom and equality."
> –Kasha Nabagesera

Kasha Nabagesera. Martin Ennals Foundation

2015 Pride March in New York City's
Greenwich Village.
DanielBendjy/iStock.com

HOW YOU CAN HELP

Both locally and globally, there are things that you can do
to help. Here are a few (and if you've just read this book,
you've already begun the first one on the list!):

Educate yourself about LGBTQ rights. There are some
resources at the end of this book that you might find helpful.

Be an ally. Let your family, friends and teachers know
that you support equality for LGBTQ people—both where
you live and around the world.

Speak up for equality! Take a stand against discrimination whenever you see it.

Fight bullying. Challenge anti-gay jokes, comments
and stereotypes.

Join the Gay-Straight Alliance at your school. If your
school doesn't have a GSA, think about taking steps to

change that! For information about how to start a GSA at your school, check out this website: www.gsanetwork.org/get-involved/start-gsa.

Use your power as a consumer. Don't give your money to companies that oppose LGBTQ rights. Do support queer-positive organizations, and do watch TV shows and movies that include queer characters—better ratings will lead to more queer content. And buy diverse books or ask your local library to get them! The American Library Association's Rainbow List is a great place to find books with LGBTQ characters.

Write letters to the media and to elected officials, letting them know that you support equal rights for LGBTQ people. Sign petitions supporting equality and challenging human rights abuses. If you or your family can afford to, consider supporting ILGA or Amnesty International—or donate directly to one of the many small queer activist organizations, like Freedom and Roam Uganda.

And finally, don't forget about Pride Day! Come on out, show your support, and celebrate equality, diversity and freedom with LGBTQ people and their allies. Be a part of it!

2015 San Francisco Pride Parade. ffennema/iStock.com

Pride parade, Copenhagen, Denmark, 2014.
Laubelstockphoto/Dreamstime.com

GLOSSARY

ableism—the belief that able-bodied people are normal and people with disabilities are inferior, and the resulting exclusion of and/or discrimination against individuals with disabilities

ally—a person who supports the rights and freedoms of a marginalized or oppressed group that he or she is not a part of

asexual—a person who is generally not sexually attracted to anyone and feels little or no sexual desire

bisexual—a person who is attracted to both men and women

cisgender—people whose gender identity matches the sex they were assigned at birth

classism—discrimination against people because of their perceived social or economic class; also refers to the system of beliefs and structures that disadvantages some social classes while unfairly benefiting others

coming out—the process LGBTQ people go through as they move toward understanding, accepting and being more open about their gender identity or sexual orientation

discrimination—actions or decisions that treat a person or a group negatively because of their perceived race, sex, age, sexual orientation, gender identity, gender expression, religion or disability

drag—when clothing typical of one sex is worn by a person of the opposite sex

dyke march—a political demonstration that aims to increase visibility for lesbians and transgender people and all women who love women, however they identify themselves

equality—the state of having the same rights, freedoms, social status, etc.

gay—a person who is attracted primarily to members of the same sex

genderfluid—a term used to describe a gender identity that shifts from day to day

gender identity—an internal sense of one's gender (male, female, non-binary)

gender neutral—a person who doesn't identify as either male or female

genderqueer—a person whose gender identity lies outside traditional binary ideas of masculine and feminine; also known as non-binary

heterosexism—the system of beliefs and attitudes based on the idea that everyone is or should be attracted to the opposite sex, and the resulting prejudice and discrimination against LGBTQ people

homophobia—the fear or hatred of people who are gay, lesbian or bisexual

intersex—a person whose physical sex (their body, their chromosomes and their hormones) doesn't fit easily into traditional categories of male or female

labrys—a double-headed ax from ancient Crete, representing lesbian and feminist strength

lambda—a Greek letter used in many countries as a symbol of the gay and lesbian community

lesbian—a woman who is primarily attracted to other women

LGBT—stands for lesbian, gay, bisexual and transgender

LGBTQ—stands for lesbian, gay, bisexual, transgender and queer

LGBTTIQQ2SA—stands for lesbian, gay, bisexual, transgender, transsexual, intersex, queer, questioning, two-spirited and asexual

non-binary—see genderqueer

oppression—mistreatment and exploitation of a group of people based on their race, class, sexual orientation, ability, etc.; usually linked to a prevailing belief that the target group is in some way inferior

pansexual—a person attracted to all genders, recognizing that not everyone identifies as a man or a woman

persecution—the act of treating someone cruelly or unfairly, especially because of race, gender and religious or political beliefs

queer—a term sometimes used by LGBTQ people to refer to all those whose gender identity or sexual orientation falls outside the dominant heterosexual and gender-conforming mainstream

queer-positive—a term used to describe a person, organization or event that supports LGBTQ rights

questioning—a term referring to people who may not currently identify as LGBTQ but are in the process of exploring and discovering their sexual orientation, gender identity or gender expression

QUILTBAG—an acronym for queer/questioning, undecided, intersex, lesbian, trans (transgender/transsexual), bisexual, asexual and gay

racism— the system of beliefs and attitudes that holds whiteness to be superior, and the resulting oppression of people of color

sexism—the system of beliefs and attitudes that holds men to be superior, and the resulting oppression of women

sexual orientation—the pattern of a person's romantic and sexual attractions to other people; an individual may be primarily attracted to members of the opposite sex, members of their own sex, to both men and women, or toward people of multiple genders

transgender—a term often used to refer to people who do not identify with their assigned gender at birth

transitioning—the process of socially and/or physically changing from male to female or female to male

trans march—a political demonstration that aims to increase visibility, awareness and acceptance of transgender people

transphobia—fear or hatred of transgender people

transsexual—a term used by some transgender people who have transitioned from male to female or female to male

two-spirited (2S)—a term used by some First Nations people to refer to a person who has both a masculine and a feminine spirit; sometimes used as a broader term to include same-sex attraction and a wide variety of gender identities and expressions

REFERENCES

CHAPTER ONE

Apuzzo, Virginia M. and Martha Shelley. "Stonewall Participants." Accessed at http://www.pbs.org/wgbh/americanexperience/features/biography/stonewall-participants/

Cohen, Stephen. *The Gay Liberation Youth Movement in New York: An Army of Lovers Cannot Fail.* New York, NY: Routledge, 2009.

Duberman, Martin. *Stonewall.* New York, NY: Penguin, 1993.

Faderman, Lillian. *Odd Girls and Twilight Lovers: A History of Lesbian Life in Twentieth-Century America.* New York, NY: Penguin, 1991.

"The Gay Divide." Article in *The Economist.* October 11, 2014.

Marcus, Eric. *Making Gay History*: *The Half-Century Fight for Lesbian and Gay Equal Rights.* New York, NY: HarperCollins, 2002.

McCarthy, Justin. "Same-Sex Marriage Support Reaches New High at 55%." *Gallup.* May 21, 2014. Accessed at http://www.gallup.com/poll/169640/sex-marriage-support-reaches-new-high.aspx

Monette, Paul. *Borrowed Time: An AIDS Memoir.* Orlando, FL: Harcourt Brace and Company, 1998.

CHAPTER TWO

Coyote, Ivan E., and Spoon, Rae. *Gender Failure.* Vancouver, BC: Arsenal Pulp Press, 2014.

Hernandez, Daisy. "Choose Your Words With Cuidado." In *Fifty Ways to Support Lesbian and Gay Equality,* ed. Meredith Maran and Angela Watrous. Novato, CA: New World Library, 2005.

Hoad, Neville Wallace, Karen Martin and Graham Reid. *Sex and Politics in South Africa.* Cape Town: Double Storey Books, 2010.

Holliday, Ian. "11-Year-Old Transgender Girl Not Done Yet After Changing Birth Certificate." Article for CTV News, July 23, 2014. Accessed at http://bc.ctvnews.ca/11-year-old-transgender-girl-not-done-yet-after-changing-birth-certificate-1.1929208

Sheldon, Mia, and Jill Krop. "10-Year-Old Transgender Child Fights to Have Gender Removed From Birth Certificate." Article in *Global News*, December 7, 2013. Accessed at http://globalnews.ca/news/1008919/10-year-old-transgender-child-fights-to-have-gender-removed-from-birth-certificate

CHAPTER THREE

Ascah, Adrienne. "Universalist Muslims Embrace Queer Brothers and Sisters." Article in *Daily Xtra*, July 22, 2014. Accessed at http://dailyxtra.com/ottawa/news/universalist-muslims-embrace-queer-brothers-and-sisters-89649

Brachear, Manya A. "Pride Parade to Put Faith at the Forefront." Article in *Chicago Tribune*, June 24, 2012. Accessed at http://articles.chicagotribune.com/2012-06-24/news/ct-met-gay-pride-parade-religion-20120624_1_pride-parade-religious-groups-gay-community

CHAPTER FOUR

Beyond Gay: The Politics of Pride. Documentary directed by Bob Christie. USA, 2010.

Cleo. "Cleo's Moments of Pride." Article in *Bombastic: Our Voices, Our Stories, Our Lives*. 2014. Accessed at http://www.kuchutimes.com/bombastic-magazine-online-edition

Dougherty, Sarah. "These Are the 6 Openly Gay Athletes Competing at the Sochi Olympics." Article in *Global Post*, February 5, 2014. Accessed at http://www.globalpost.com/dispatch/news/regions/europe/russia/140203/6-openly-gay-athletes-sochi-olympics-russia

Free and Equal: United Nations Campaign for LGBT Equality. Accessed at https://www.unfe.org/en

Jacqueline, Kasha. "The Attack on Gay Rights in Uganda." Article in *Oslo Freedom Forum*, September 28, 2012. Accessed at https://oslofreedomforum.com/speakers/kasha-jacqueline

"Kasha Nabagesera." Article for *Wikipedia*. Accessed at http://en.wikipedia.org/wiki/Kasha_Nabagesera

Lavers, Michael K. "US to Ban Uganda Officials for LGBT Rights Abuses." Article in *The Washington Blade*, June 19, 2014. Accessed at http://www.washingtonblade.com/2014/06/19/u-s-ban-uganda-officials-lgbt-rights-abuses/

Nelson, Sarah C. "Lesbian Muslim Iranians Sahar Mosleh & Maryam Iranfar Have Marriage Blessed By Gay Imam In Sweden." Article in *The Huffington Post UK*, August 28, 2014. Accessed at http://www.huffingtonpost.co.uk/2014/08/20/lesbian-muslim-iranians-sahar-mosleh-maryam-iranfar-marriage-blessed-gay-imam-sweden_n_5694050.html

Okeowo, Alexis. "Gay and Proud in Uganda." *The New Yorker*, August 6, 2012. Accessed at http://www.newyorker.com/newsdesk/gay-and-proud-in-uganda

Onziema, Pepe Julian. "My Pride Story." Article in *Bombastic: Our Voices, Our Stories, Our Lives*. 2014. Accessed at www.kuchutimes.com/bombastic-magazine-online-edition

"Tens of Thousands Turn Out for Istanbul Gay Pride Parade." Article in *The New Paper*, June 30, 2014. Accessed at http://www.tnp.sg/news/tens-thousands-turn-out-istanbul-gay-pride-parade

"Thousands March in Seoul for S. Korea's Gay Pride Parade." Article in *Channel NewsAsia*, June 28, 2015. Accessed at www.channelnewsasia.com/news/asiapacific/thousands-march-in-seoul/1946262.html

Titi-Fontaine, Sandra. "Gay Rights Activist Calls For End to Hate." Article for *swissinfo.ch*, October 14, 2011. Accessed at http://www.swissinfo.ch/eng/gay-rights-activist-calls-for-end-to-hate/31349340

Zakharova, Svetlana. "Biggest ever LGBT public demonstration in Russia for IDAHOT." Article for *The Idaho Committee*. Accessed at http://dayagainsthomophobia.org/biggest-ever-lgbt-public-demonstration-in-russia-for-idahot/

RESOURCES

BOOKS

Bausum, Ann. *Stonewall: Breaking Out in the Fight for Gay Rights*. New York, NY: Penguin, 2015.

Carroll, Aengus and Lucas Paoli Itaborahy. *State-Sponsored Homophobia*, 10th ed. ILGA (International Lesbian, Gay, Bisexual, Trans and Intersex Association), May 2015. PDF accessed at http://old.ilga.org/Statehomophobia/ ILGA_State_Sponsored_ Homophobia_2015.pdf

Coyote, Ivan E. *One in Every Crowd*. Vancouver, BC: Arsenal Pulp Press, 2012.

Huegel, Kelly. *GLBTQ: The Survival Guide for Queer and Questioning Teens*. Minneapolis, MN: FreeSpirit Publishing, 2011.

Kuklin, Susan. *Beyond Magenta*. Somerville, MS: Candlewick Press, 2014.

Marcus, Eric. *What if Someone I Know Is Gay? Answers to Questions about Gay and Lesbian People*. New York, NY: Simon and Schuster, 2007.

Moon, Sarah, and James Lecesne, eds. *The Letter Q: Queer Writers' Notes to Their Younger Selves*. New York, NY: Scholastic Inc., 2014.

Savage, Dan, and Terry Miller, eds. *It Gets Better: Coming Out, Overcoming Bullying, and Creating a Life Worth Living*. New York, NY: Penguin, 2012.

Setterington, Ken. *Branded by the Pink Triangle*. Toronto, ON: Second Story Press, 2013.

WEBSITES

American Library Association's Annual Rainbow List of recommended books with LGBTQ content:
www.glbtrt.ala.org/rainbowbooks/rainbow-books-lists

Free and Equal: United Nations Campaign for LGBT Equality:
www.unfe.org/en

Gay-Straight Alliance Network:
US site: www.gsanetwork.org
Canadian site: www.mygsa.ca

Support and Information for LGBTQ Youth:
The Trevor Project: www.thetrevorproject.org
It Gets Better Campaign: www.itgetsbetter.org

Support and Information for Youth, Parents, Families and Friends:
PFLAG National (USA): www.community.pflag.org
PFLAG Canada: www.pflagcanada.ca

INDEX

*Page numbers in **bold** indicate an image; there may also be text related to the same topic on that page*

Me at Victoria Pride Day 2015, with a wonderful group of Pride supporters and allies of all ages. Some of the teens in this group are in the process of starting a Gay-Straight Alliance for homeschoolers.
Robin Stevenson

ACKNOWLEDGMENTS

Some of the best parts of writing this book were the conversations I had with the many wonderful and generous people who were willing to help. Thank you to every person—far too many to list—who took the time to speak with me and share their thoughts about Pride.

For helpful and thought-provoking discussions, and for their astute comments on early drafts, many thanks to Khalilah Alwani, Rachel Hope Cleves, Maya Ann Cleves, Kari Jones, Carrie Mac and Dylan Schoenmakers.

For sharing their stories and photographs, I am very grateful to Elena Abel; Aiden and Maia Cassie; Natasha Coldevin; Harriette, Megan and Colin Cunningham; Emily and Stephanie Faulkner; Ryan Marc Jackson; Amanda Littauer; Wendy Martin and Kizea Martin-Hanson;

Lauren Moses-Brettler; Samuel Murray; Kasha Nabagesera; Pidgeon Pagonis; Amanda Saenz; Duncan Smith; Trudy Spiller and Tanisha; Amy Stewart; Carl Swanson; Shelley Taylor and Gart Van Gennip. Many thanks also to Rich Wandel at The Lesbian, Gay, Bisexual and Transgender Community Center National History Archives in New York City for his assistance and for sharing many of the wonderful archival photographs that appear in these pages. Thanks to all the Pride event organizers, from the Victoria Pride Society here in my hometown to the staff and volunteers of the Sydney Mardi Gras in Australia, who answered my questions and shared their photographs. I am also grateful to Emily Quinn of Inter/Act Youth for helping me to make sure the "I" in LGBTQIA was represented. And finally, a great big thank-you to every single person—and there are too many of you to list here—who helped make this book a reality.

For stunning photography, thanks to all the talented individuals whose images brought this book to life. To Tony Sprackett, brilliant photographer and fellow Fernwood resident: sitting down with you and looking through your beautiful photographs helped this book take shape in my mind, and I am tremendously grateful for all your help.

For her enthusiasm for the idea of a book about Pride, and for being a terrific guide for my first foray into nonfiction, I am very grateful to my fabulous editor and friend, Sarah Harvey. For all her creativity, enthusiasm and attention to detail, thanks to designer Rachel Page—you made this book so beautiful. And for everyone in the Orca pod, thank you so much for all your support. I couldn't be luckier.

A NOTE FROM THE AUTHOR

The pace of change in the last few years has been incredible—and it seemed to accelerate while I was writing this book. For example, Mozambique and Palau decriminalized homosexuality, Ireland voted to accept same-sex marriage, and the Supreme Court legalized same-sex marriage across the United States. In every case, I was delighted to revise the text to reflect this progress! But at some point, revisions must stop and books must go to press—and by the time this book reaches readers' hands, it may already be out of date. While there will no doubt be challenges ahead for the LGBTQ community, I have great confidence that our diverse, passionate, courageous and creative community will continue to fight for freedom and equality—and that changes for the better will continue to happen.

WHAT MAKES ORCA'S NONFICTION DIFFERENT?

Whether the topic is sustainability, cultural celebrations or activism for kids, our books are
passion projects.

Written by enthusiastic authors who are keen to share their experiences, research and life's work with young readers, Orca's nonfiction is ready to make a splash!